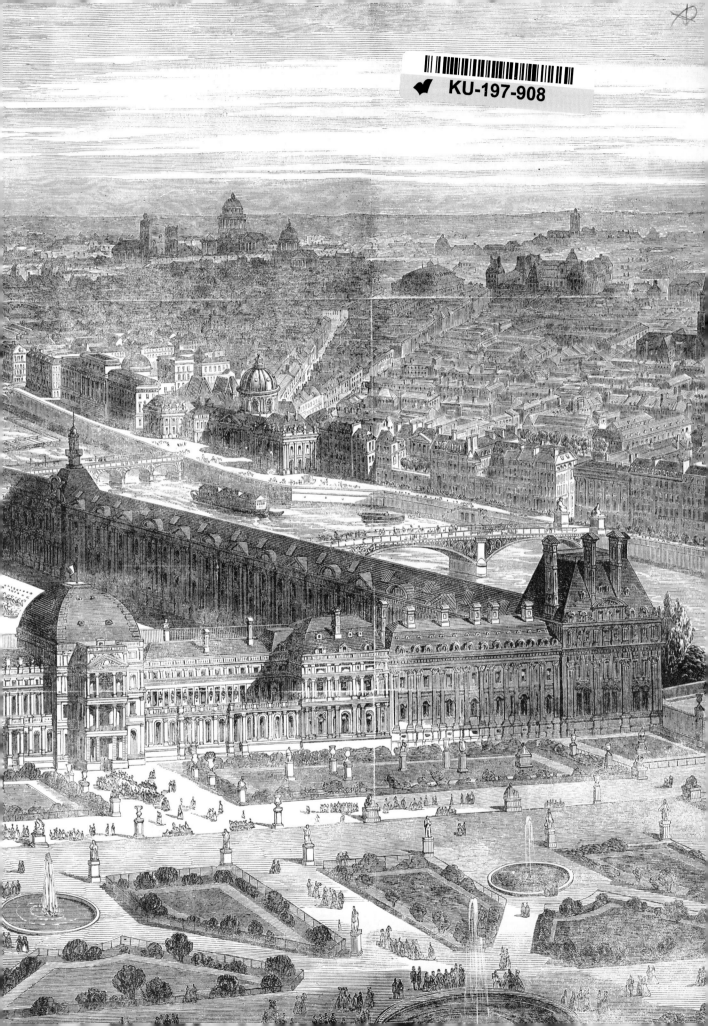

MICHEL LACLOTTE
Director, Department of Paintings

JEAN-PIERRE CUZIN
Keeper, Department of Paintings

THE LOUVRE

French and other European paintings

Scala/Philip Wilson

© 1982 Editions Scala, Paris and Philip Wilson Publishers Ltd, London

First published 1982 by
Philip Wilson Publishers Ltd and Summerfield Press Ltd
Russell Chambers, Covent Garden, London WC2E 8AA

Text: Michel Laclotte and Jean-Pierre Cuzin
Translated from the French by Diana de Froment and Frances Roxburgh
Photographs: Hubert Josse
Design: Richard Johnson
Edited by Philip Wilson Publishers Ltd, London
Series Editor: Judy Spours

Phototypeset by Tradespools Ltd, Frome, Somerset
Produced by Scala Istituto Fotografico Editoriale, Firenze
Printed in Italy

ISBN 0 85667 147 9

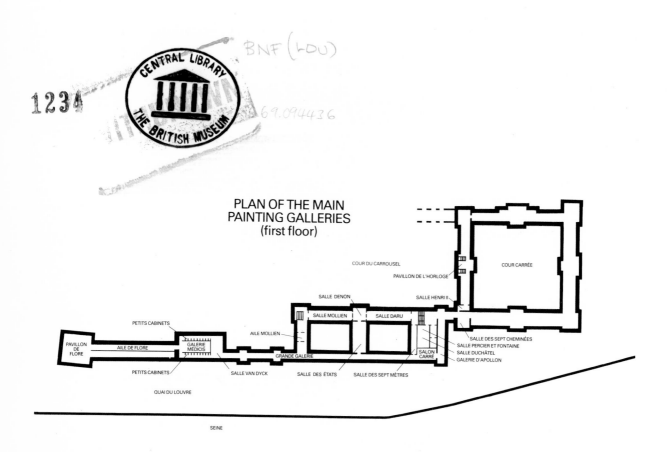

PLAN OF THE MAIN
PAINTING GALLERIES
(first floor)

COUR DU CARROUSEL

COUR CARRÉE

PAVILLON DE L'HORLOGE

SALLE DENON

SALLE HENRI II

SALLE MOLLIEN

SALLE DARU

AILE MOLLIEN

SALLE DES SEPT CHEMINÉES
SALLE PERCIER ET FONTAINE
SALLE DUCHÂTEL
GALERIE D'APOLLON

PETITS CABINETS

GALERIE
MÉDICIS

PAVILLON
DE
FLORE

AILE DE FLORE

GRANDE GALERIE

SALON
CARRÉ

PETITS CABINETS

SALLE VAN DYCK

SALLE DES ÉTATS

SALLE DES SEPT MÉTRES

QUAI DU LOUVRE

SEINE

The Publishers would like to thank Documentation Française Photothèque for
their permission to reproduce the engraving on p. viii

Front cover: Raphael, *Balthasar Castiglione, circa* 1514/15 (detail)
Back cover: Watteau, *The pilgrimage to Cythera,* 1717 (detail)

Contents

Chronology of principal dates in the history of the building of the Louvre and the creation of the Museum

1180–1223 PHILIPPE AUGUSTE
1190
Under Philippe Auguste the keep and defensive walls of the Louvre are built on a site which is now the south-west corner of the Cour Carrée.

1214
The keep is used to house the royal treasure, archives and furniture store, and also as a prison.

1364–80 CHARLES V
1365–70
Under Charles V the château is extended to the north and east; the keep is now entirely surrounded by buildings. It is sometimes used as a royal residence but the court is based in the Hôtel Saint Paul to the east of Paris.

1515–47 FRANÇOIS I
1527
François I decides to make the Louvre his official residence; destruction of the keep.

1546
At the end of his reign François I commissions Pierre Lescot to rebuild the Louvre. The King's collection of paintings is to stay in the Château de Fontainebleau until the middle of the seventeenth century.

1547–59 HENRI II
1547–49
Under Henri II the Aile de Lescot is completed (south part of what is now the west wing of the Cour Carrée), decorated by the sculptor Jean Goujon; the Pavillon du Roi is built on the site which is now the Salle des Sept Cheminées.

1559–60 FRANÇOIS II
1560–74 CHARLES IX
1559–74
Continuation of work on what is now the south of the Cour Carrée.

1564–74
Catherine de Médicis commissions Philibert Delorme to build a château outside the walls of Paris, called the Tuileries.

1566
Construction of the Petite Galerie (now the Galerie d'Apollon).

1574–89 HENRI III
1589–1610 HENRI IV
1595–1610
Under Henri IV, the Grande Galerie is built, designed by Louis Metezeau and Jacques II Androuet du Cerceau, and the new Château des Tuileries is linked to the Vieux Louvre.

1610–43 LOUIS XIII
1624–54
Under Louis XIII the Pavillon de l'Horloge is designed by Jacques Lemercier. It is attached to the Aile de Lescot, and to balance this wing another symmetrical one is built to the north.

1641–42
Nicolas Poussin is commissioned to decorate the vaulted ceiling of the Grande Galerie with scenes from the life of Hercules; after initial plans the project is abandoned.

1643–1715 LOUIS XIV
1659–65
Louis Le Vau builds the north and south wings of the Cour Carrée.

1661–70
Le Vau builds the Galerie d'Apollon after the fire in the Galerie des Rois, on the first floor of the Petite Galerie.

1664–66
Le Vau and François d'Orbay make major changes and enlargements to the Château des Tuileries.

1667–70
The Colonnade, the eastern façade of the Louvre, is designed by Le Vau, d'Orbay and Claude Perrault. The façade by Le Vau to the south is concealed by a new one designed to be in keeping with the Colonnade.

1674
Works on the Louvre abandoned; from 1678 to 1789 the Château de Versailles is to be the residence of the King and Court. Organised almost like a museum, the royal collection of paintings is brought together in the Louvre and the Hôtel de Gramont attached to it. Gradually the pictures are distributed to the various royal residences.

1715–74 LOUIS XV
from 1725
The official exhibition of the Académie Royale de Peinture et Sculpture takes place in the Salon Carré of the Louvre, from which comes the name 'Salon'. These Salons took place until 1848.

from 1754
Jacques Ange Gabriel undertakes transformation of the second floor of the Cour Carrée.

1755
Public exhibition at the Palais du Luxembourg of a selection of paintings from the royal collection.

1755–74
Demolition of the old residential area around the Cour Carrée and Colonnade.

1774–92 LOUIS XVI
1774
The Comte d'Angiviller becomes Surintendant des Bâtiments du Roi; studies and projects for the creation of a 'Muséum' in the Grande Galerie.

1777
The 'plans and models' of royal châteaux which filled the Grande Galerie are cleared away.

1784
Hubert Robert, Conservateur des collections du Roi, is given responsibility for the organisation of the 'Muséum'. Top lighting installed in the Salon Carrée. The King once again lives in Paris: Louis XVI resides in the Château des Tuileries.

1789
Outbreak of the French Revolution.

1791–92
After the French Revolution the royal collection becomes the national collection. Seizures of works of art from churches, convents and the nobility. A committee of artists continues the preparations for the opening of the 'Muséum'.

1793
The Muséum Central des Arts is opened. A 'special museum for French painting' is instituted in the Château de Versailles.

1796–1807
An enormous influx of works of art into the Louvre, surrendered by or commandeered from Holland, Italy and Germany during the Napoleonic wars.

1800
Napoleon Bonaparte moves into the Château des Tuileries.

1802–15
Vivant Denon Director of the museum which, in 1803, is renamed the Musée Napoléon.

1804
Napoleon is crowned Emperor.

1806
Construction of the Arc de Triomphe du Carrousel, the monumental gateway to the Château des Tuileries designed by Percier and Fontaine.

1810–14
Construction of the north wing of the Louvre along the rue de Rivoli, also designed by Percier and Fontaine.

1814–24 LOUIS XVIII
1815
After the Battle of Waterloo all the works of art that had been surrendered by or commandeered from foreign countries are returned, except about a hundred paintings, mostly Italian, which stay in the Louvre.

1818
The Galerie royale du Luxembourg is created exclusively for the display of work by contemporary artists (subsequently the Musée du Luxembourg).

1824–30 CHARLES X
1827
The Musée Charles X is created in the southern wing of the Cour Carrée.

1830–48 LOUIS-PHILIPPE
1838
Inauguration of Louis-Philippe's Musée Espagnol in the eastern wing of the Cour Carrée.

1848–70 NAPOLEON III
1848
The Second Republic decides to complete the Louvre as a 'palace of the people' devoted to the sciences and arts. Restoration and redecoration by Duban; Eugène Delacroix commissioned to execute the ceiling painting for the vault of the Galerie d'Apollon.

1851
Inauguration of the new rooms.

1852
Baron Haussmann orders the demolition of the old residential area between the Château des Tuileries and the Louvre.

1852–57
Construction of the 'new Louvre' by Louis-Tulluis Visconti and later Hector Lefuel; the two palaces are linked together to the north by a series of buildings, thus closing the square with the Arc du Carrousel at the centre. New wings are constructed on either side of the Cour Napoléon producing large courtyards and allowing top lighting to be installed.

1861–70
Reconstruction by Lefuel of the Pavillon de Flore, decorated by Jean-Baptiste Carpeaux, and the western end of the Grande Galerie. The monumental triple arch through the southern wing is constructed.

1871
During the Commune (March–May) the administration of the museum is undertaken by a group of artists, including Gustave Courbet, Honoré Daumier and Félix Bracquemond.
The Château des Tuileries is burnt out; the shell is not demolished until 1883 when the view from the Arc du Carrousel to the Arc de Triomphe is revealed.

1895
The Réunion des Musées Nationaux is created with autonomous financial powers respecting purchases. It is run by the Conseil des Musées Nationaux.

1897
Foundation of the Société des Amis du Louvre.

1927
Under the authority of Henri Verne, Directeur des musées, a vast plan to reorganise the collection is begun. The decoration of the Grande Galerie is completed using Hubert Robert's designs.

from 1945
The collection is brought back having been evacuated during the war and the exhibition rooms are gradually reopened.

1953
Installation of Georges Braque's triple composition *The birds* in the ceiling of the Salle Henri II replacing that by Merry-Joseph Blondel (1822).

1961
The galleries for nineteenth-century art are opened on the second floor of the Cour Carrée.

1969–71
The galleries in the Pavillon de Flore and the Aile de Flore are opened.

1971
The first of a series of documentary exhibitions, 'Files from the Département des Peintures'.

1972
A law is instigated allowing the presentation of works of art in lieu of death duties.

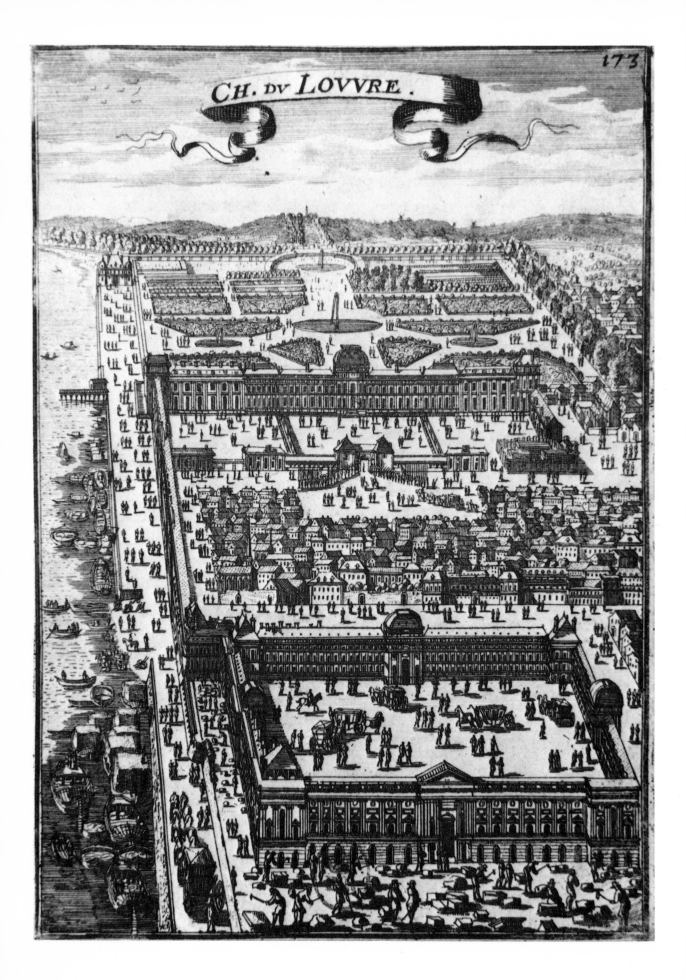

CH. DV LOVVRE.

French paintings in the Louvre

Anonymous, *View of the palais du Louvre and Château des Tuileries in the seventeenth century*, late seventeenth/early eighteenth century

GIUSEPPE CASTIGLIONE, *View of the Salon Carré in 1861*, 1861

The Salon Carré, at the eastern end of the Grande Galerie, is one of the most famous rooms in the Louvre. The official exhibitions of contemporary French paintings mounted by the Académie Royale de Peinture et de Sculpture were held here from their inception at the beginning of the eighteenth century until the mid-nineteenth century. It was this tradition that gave rise to the name 'Salon' for temporary exhibitions of paintings. Castiglione's painting shows the room just after 1851 when it had been redecorated and given a sumptuous new ceiling by Duban and Simart. The Salons now took place elsewhere and the dense display of paintings in this picture comprises a selection of the most renowned masterpieces in the Louvre at the time—all schools of painting and periods mixed together. Today the Salon Carré is devoted entirely to French fifteenth- and sixteenth-century art.

Introduction

The French paintings in the Louvre represent well over half the Museum's entire collection; their quality and fame make them by far the most important extant collection of such works. It was therefore decided to divide the Louvre's great paintings into two parts, and that the first of them should be devoted solely to the French School. It should, however, be emphasised that the Museum's other collections, such as the Italian, could well have merited this preeminence, since chronologically the scope of these two parts does not go much beyond the middle of the nineteenth century and, therefore, excludes the Impressionists and Post-Impressionists. The second part, *European Paintings in the Louvre*, covers the Museum's wealth of works from countries other than France and with the first provides for the reader a balanced view of the collection as a whole. In the following pages we shall trace the history of the Louvre itself and of its unique range of French paintings from the beginning of the sixteenth century to the end of the twentieth. Apart from Watteau in the Wallace Collection in London and in Berlin-Charlottenburg, and Bourdon in the Hermitage in Leningrad, there is scarcely any French artist that can be more fully studied elsewhere than in the Louvre.

We know that François I brought artists from Italy to decorate the Château de Fontainebleau and that he collected Italian paintings. He chose works by Leonardo da Vinci rather than contemporary ones by French artists, such as the Master of Moulins. Probably the only French paintings we would have found in the royal collection would have been family portraits. One still exists and is preserved in the Louvre—the portrait of François I himself, attributed to Jean Clouet (p. 18), which has now become the symbol of the continuity of the Louvre, a national collection which grew out of the royal collection.

It was not until the reign of Henri IV, after a long period of civil war, that another king was interested in art and commissioned paintings: some of those by Dubreuil which decorated the Château Neuf, Saint-Germain-en-Laye, have survived (p. 24), but we can really only talk about vestiges of a decorative scheme rather than a collection of paintings. Louis XIII commissioned works from Simon Vouet and asked Nicolas Poussin to decorate the Grande Galerie in the Louvre, as well as commissioning a large altar-piece from him (p. 38), although Louis XIII was not really a collector.

It was Louis XIV who enthusiastically resumed the traditional rôle of patron of the arts that had been established by François I. His reign saw the true beginnings of the Louvre's collection of French paintings, and it was dominated by four contemporary artists, two living in Rome, Poussin and Claude, and the King's two official painters, Le Brun and Mignard. After the death of Cardinal Mazarin in 1661, 546 of the former Prime Minister's most beautiful paintings became part of the King's collection. Of these 77 were French, although unfortunately their titles are not known. Throughout Louis XIV's reign many marvellous works by Poussin and Claude were bought or given to the king. Le Brun, Garde des tableaux du Roi until his death, prepared the first inventory of the royal collection in 1683 and another more systematic one was produced by the miniaturist Bailly in 1710. He catalogued 2,376 paintings of which 898 were copies, anonymous, of dubious attribution, or by Le Brun, Verdier and Mignard. Of the 1,478 paintings which constituted the main collection, the vast majority were French. Many, however, were not easel paintings but decorative works for the royal châteaux. The Cabinet du Roi (the King's art collection) was in the new part of the Louvre created by Le Vau, but these paintings were gradually dispersed to Versailles and other royal residences.

Louis xv, unlike his contemporaries the King of Prussia, the German princes, the Tsarina and the Queen of Sweden, was not a great lover of paintings; in 1770 the fabulous Crozat collection belonging to Baron de Thiers was sold in its entirety to Catherine the Great of Russia. Apart from a few paintings purchased from the Carignan estate, the royal collection was augmented only by canvases or tapestry cartoons commissioned to decorate the royal residences. Nevertheless, this means that the Louvre now owns important paintings by Boucher, Lancret, Vernet, Oudry, Van Loo and Fragonard.

On the other hand, it was during Louis xv's reign that it was decided to show part of the royal collection to artists and the public, a real innovation. From 1750–79, 110 paintings were exhibited in rooms in the Palais du Luxembourg, open at the same time as Rubens' Galerie Médicis, two half-days a week. Among the canvases displayed in this embryo museum, forerunner of the Louvre's, were a variety of French paintings—eleven by Poussin, four each by Claude and Valentin, and one or two each by Vouet, Le Sueur, Le Brun, Rigaud, Antoine and Noël Coypel, Mignard, La Fosse, Santerre, Vivien and Lemoyne.

Louis xvi's reign was decisive for the royal collection and would certainly have seen the opening of the Louvre museum had it not been for the French Revolution. In 1774, the year of the King's accession to the throne, the Comte d'Angiviller became Surintendant des Bâtiments du Roi, an appointment which included control of the royal collection. He realised the rôle that earlier masterpieces could play in 'reviving' French painting and to this end planned to open a 'Muséum' in the Grande Galerie of the Louvre. He tried to fill the gaps in the collection and systematically ordered works to be reframed in an attempt to unify the paintings. This constituted the birth in France of modern theories of museum conservation and display. French paintings were often purchased: not only history paintings commissioned from contemporaries, but also earlier seventeenth-century works, notably the cycle depicting the life of St. Bruno by Le Sueur.

The Muséum Central des Arts finally opened in the summer of 1793, during the Convention. Louis xvi's collection became that of the nation, and the revolutionary leaders, despite enormous immediate difficulties, were sufficiently enthusiastic to bring to fruition an enterprise that had begun under the monarchy. The concept of the museum, which had been growing throughout Europe, now came to fruition. At the Louvre, however, its realisation took on proportions which no-one could have dreamed of during the Ancien Régime. To the royal collection were added vast numbers of works seized from churches, convents and the nobility, as well as the works which had constituted the collection of the Académie Royale de Peinture et de Sculpture. A museum committee, consisting chiefly of artists, decided which works to keep for the Louvre. When the museum opened the paintings were hung in a very surprising mixture of periods and schools. Among the French paintings were several by Le Sueur and Vernet, examples by Poussin, Vouet, Patel, Champaigne, Valentin, Dughet, Bourdon, Mignard, Jouvenet and Desportes, two by Trémolières, a small Subleyras, a Vignon (now in Grenoble) and even a work by Tournier, then attributed to Manfredi (now in Le Mans). The earliest French painting was *The Last Judgement* by Jean Cousin the Younger, which had come from the convent of the Minimes, Vincennes.

So many works had now been gathered together that from 1793 a second museum had to be instigated at the Château de Versailles. This was the Musée Special de l'école Française, where in particular the election pieces of past and present Academicians were featured. The account of 1802 mentions 352 pictures: twenty-three by Poussin, ten by Le Brun and seven by Mignard, also examples by Vouet, Bourdon, the cycle by Le Sueur, Claude, La Fosse, Subleyras, Jouvenet, Rigaud, Chardin, Doyen, Tocqué, Van Loo, Lagrenée and Vernet. Among the contemporaries were Fragonard, Greuze and Vien. In 1804 this short-lived museum was disbanded.

However, the enormous assemblage of paintings in depots and in the Louvre was only the beginning. The victorious armies of the Republic and then the Empire commandeered the most prestigious works of art from royal collections and religious establishments throughout Europe, notably from Italy and, later, Germany. During the Empire Vivant Denon was the organiser and overseer of this unique museum. Thus, for a short time the Muséum, which had become the Musée Napoléon, owned a great part of Europe's heritage. It is interesting to note that at this stage the amount of space given to French paintings was small. In the Grande Galerie four bays were devoted to Northern Schools, four to Italian, but only one to the French.

After the Battle of Waterloo the Napoleonic dream evaporated and most of the booty in the museum was returned to its places of origin. Although the Louvre was singularly depleted, this dismantling was not fatal to the collection for, attached to the Civil List, the parliamentary allowance for sovereign's expenditure, it became once again the direct concern of the King. During the reign of Louis XVIII many of the works seized from the nobility and churches were retained by the Louvre, now seen as a great national institution. From this time on the collection turned more towards French painting; from the Palais du Luxembourg, at the same time as the Médicis series by Rubens, came the St. Bruno cycle by Le Sueur and several of Vernet's *Ports of France*. Some contemporary canvases were also purchased (David, Girodet, Guérin), and housed in the Musée du Luxembourg, which had been opened in 1818 for the works of living artists.

The most important project during the reign of Louis-Philippe was the formation of the Musée historique de Versailles, and the Louvre was somewhat abandoned. However, after the brief Republic of 1848, when it was again proposed, as it had been during the Revolution, to turn the Louvre into a 'palace of the people' including the museum, the Bibliothèque Nationale and temporary exhibition space, the Second Empire was to see one of the greatest epochs in the history of the museum. With the impetus of the Emperor behind the project, the vast Tuileries/Louvre ensemble was completed in record time, including the gigantic painting galleries (Salle Mollien, Salle Daru and Salle des États) which were such a novelty. Of the highly valuable acquisitions made during this period, the Denor La Caze collection in 1869 was the most important. Comprising some eight hundred paintings, it was the finest collection ever bequeathed to the Louvre. La Caze's contribution was inestimable in the field of French seventeenth- and eighteenth-century painting; one cannot imagine how, without him, the work of Largillière, Watteau, Chardin or Fragonard would have been represented today.

With the declaration of the Republic the Louvre became France's national museum and has remained so ever since; gone was the ambiguity of a museum funded by the Civil List of a sovereign. From that time on the purchase of paintings was gradual and methodical, acquisitions being made as knowledge of French painting was extended by art historical research. The generosity of collectors continued; gifts and bequests increased. It was, for example, collectors such as Thomy Thiéry (1902), Moreau-Nélaton (1906), Chauchard (1910) and Camondo (1911), whose gifts of whole rooms of paintings (often filling gaps left by official purchases) to a large extent formed the unrivalled collection of nineteenth-century art now owned by the Louvre. Also important are the collectors' contributions to early French painting such as those of: Schlichting (1914), Robert (1926), Croy (1930), Jamot (1941), Beistegui (1942), Gourgaud (1965) and Lyon (1961).

Above all, the magnificent support of the Société des Amis du Louvre, founded in 1897, has led to the acquisition of some of the greatest masterpieces of French painting, from the *Pietà d'Avignon* (1905) to La Tour's *St. Sebastian* (1979). The recent law allowing the donation of works of art in lieu of death duties has meant that major works by Champaigne, Fragonard and Courbet have been preserved for the nation.

In the near future two great projects will completely transform the presentation of French paintings in the Louvre. The first is the new Musée d'Orsay, in which will be exhibited many of the mid- and late nineteenth-century canvases now in the Louvre. The second is the rearrangement of the galleries in the Louvre itself. The second floor of the Cour Carré will show a continuous display of French paintings from the fourteenth to the nineteenth centuries, with only the vast nineteenth-century canvases in the Salles Daru, Denon and Mollien remaining where they are today. These new galleries will allow the entire wealth of the collection to be on view, particularly the huge seventeenth- and eighteenth-century paintings until now kept in the reserve collection. Since only the small canvases are normally displayed our ideas about French painting could be completely changed. The concept of French painting depends largely on what is seen in the Louvre, a concept which we at the Museum should constantly be broadening, redefining and varying, by drawing on the collection, enriching it still further and making it accessible to everyone.

The primitives and the sixteenth century

The great exhibition of 1904, devoted entirely to French primitive painting, established the importance and originality of those artists working before the sixteenth century. The study of fourteenth- and fifteenth-century Italian, Flemish and German painters had come well before that of their French contemporaries, and French works were therefore often attributed to other schools. In fact the concept of 'French primitives' scarcely existed before the twentieth century. Works by Van Eyck and Fra Angelico were exhibited in the Musée Napoléon but not those by Fouquet or Quarton, and the formation of the Louvre collection reflects the fact that in the history of taste French medieval art is very much a new arrival.

However, we should note a few paintings of prime importance that came into the national collection during the reign of Louis-Philippe. These paintings for the Château de Versailles, where the King was forming the Musée historique dedicated to 'all the glories of France', were purchased as historical documents: portraits of *Charles VII* and *Guillaume Jouvenel des Ursins* by Fouquet (pp. 12 and 13) and of *Pierre de Bourbon* by Jean Hey. Only the sitters were considered interesting and, *Charles VII* was even bought as a 'Greek work', implying that it was Byzantine! These pictures were only later transferred to the Louvre as works of art in their own right.

In the second half of the nineteenth century, just as the history of these works was beginning to be written, succeeding keepers of the collection bought new works and collectors gave others which are still among the most important in the Louvre. *The Narbonne altar-frontal* (p. 9) was purchased in 1852, in 1863 Frédéric Reiset gave *The St. Denis altar-piece* by Bellechose (p. 11) and Malouel's *Pietà* (p. 10) was bought the next year.

But it was the year 1904 which saw the real awakening of interest in French medieval art. The Louvre acquired *The Boulbon altar-piece* (p. 17), *The Paris Parlement altar-piece* (p. 15) and Jean Hey's *A donor and St. Mary Magdalen* (p. 14). The next year the great masterpiece *The Villeneuve-les-Avignon Pietà* (p. 16) was presented by the Société des Amis du Louvre. After that only occasional acquisitions were made, and the portrait of *Jean le Bon* (p. 9) was offered on extended loan from the Bibliothèque Nationale in 1925. Two extremely rare little paintings, a *Virgin* by a Burgundian master and *Charles-Orlant* by Jean Hey (p. 14), were part of the collection given by Carlos de Beistegui in 1942.

It is important to emphasise the extreme rarity of French primitives owing to their destruction during the Revolution and above all because of the late appreciation of these works by historians. This rarity makes us especially grateful for recent acquisitions such as *The Crucifixion with a Carthusian monk* by Jean de Beaumetz (p. 10) and *The Presentation of the Virgin* by Nicolas Dipre (p. 17), works by artists not previously represented in the Louvre, and *The Crucifixion* by Josse Lieferinxe (p. 17), an artist previously represented only by secondary work. Only in the Louvre can such a comprehensive collection .of these rare primitives be seen.

The collection of French sixteenth-century painting is also comparatively recent. The glorious exception is the portrait of *François I* attributed to Jean Clouet (p. 18) which has been part of the national collection ever since it was painted for its royal sitter in about 1530. The royal collection must have comprised many portraits: the inventory drawn up by Bailly in 1710 mentions '251 small portraits of the families of past kings and nobility'. All that is left in the Louvre is a small full-length depiction of Henri II, a studio copy of the painting in the Uffizi, Florence. Of great importance to the Louvre is the enormous collection of works of historical interest, mostly prints and drawings, bequeathed by Roger de Gaignières. On his death in 1716 the collection entered the Cabinet du Roi, precursor of the Bibliothèque Nationale. Gaignières seems to have had a particular preference for small sixteenth-century portraits and many now in the Louvre came originally from his collection. Some, which during the Revolution had passed into Alexandre Lenoir's Musée des Monuments Français, entered the Louvre in 1817; others were acquired later. In 1908 the Société des Amis du Louvre donated the highly important portrait of *Pierre Quthe* by François Clouet (p. 21). Of the more recent acquisitions that of Corneille de Lyon's *Pierre Aymeric* (p. 22) in 1976 is particularly significant as one of his few documented works. Also of note is the purchase in 1967 of the rare *Portrait of a couple* (p. 24). Thus the Louvre is able to exhibit a comprehensive collection of sixteenth-century portraits. Their precision and concern for the character of the sitter are derived from northern models, features which were to be the hallmarks of French portraiture, and continually developed in later centuries.

Taste for Mannerist art is more recent even than that for early portraits. The Italian artists who came to France in the sixteenth century gave rise to a complete change in taste, giving François I's court a style of painting that was elegant and decorative, very often with mythological settings. This charming Fontainebleau School, with its accent on the artificial, has only been studied during the past few decades and has only recently been represented in the Louvre. The famous *Diana, goddess of the hunt* (p. 19) was acquired for Fontainebleau during Louis-Philippe's reign because it was thought to be a portrait of Diane de Poitiers, Henri II's favourite. Apart from a few other exceptions—Gourmont's *Adoration of the shepherds*, the works by Dubreuil from the chapel of the Château d'Écouen and *The Last Judgement* by Cousin the Younger seized from the convent of the Minimes, Vincennes—the collection has been built up over the past sixty years. *Eva Prima Pandora* by Cousin the Elder (p. 18) was presented in 1922, the very popular *Gabrielle d'Estrées and one of her sisters* (p. 24) was purchased in 1937 and *Augustus and the Sybil* by Caron (p. 23) presented in 1958. Recently a great effort has been made to form a collection which will show all aspects of the Fontainebleau School, with purchases including the mid-sixteenth-century *Charity* (p. 19), in 1970, and in 1973 *The justice of Othon* attributed to Luca Penni.

SCHOOL OF PARIS, second half of the 14th century
The Narbonne altar-frontal, circa 1375
Black ink on silk   77.5 × 286 cm
Purchased in 1852

SCHOOL OF PARIS, second half of the 14th century
Jean II le Bon, King of France, circa 1360
Wood   59.8 × 44.6 cm
Extended loan from the Bibliothèque Nationale, 1925

JEAN MALOUEL
Niemegen, before 1370 – Dijon, 1415
Pietà known as '*La grande Pietà ronde*',
  circa 1400
Wood   diameter 64.5 cm
Purchased in 1864

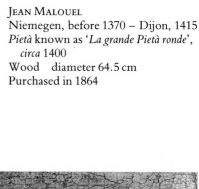

JEAN DE BEAUMETZ
Artois, first known in 1361 – Dijon, 1396
Crucifixion with a Carthusian monk, between 1389 and 1395
Wood   60 × 48.5 cm
Purchased in 1967

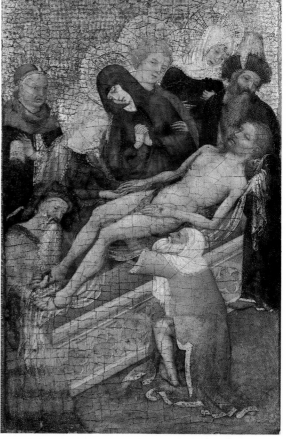

SCHOOL OF PARIS OR BURGUNDY, early 15th century
The Entombment of Christ, circa 1400
Wood   32.8 × 21.3 cm
Purchased in 1869

Henri Bellechose
Brabant, known in Dijon from 1415 – Dijon, 1440/44
The St. Denis altar-piece, finished in 1416
Wood transferred to canvas   162 × 211 cm
Presented by Frédéric Reiset, 1863

Jean de Beaumetz, Jean Malouel and Henri Bellechose, working in Dijon, were successively the official artists of the Dukes of Burgundy, Philippe le Hardi and Jean sans Peur. The Louvre is extremely fortunate in possessing a painting by each of them. Characteristic of their work is the combination of refined draughtsmanship with fresh, brilliant colours heightened by gilding, in an attempt to express deep emotion.

JEAN FOUQUET
Tours, *circa* 1420 – Tours, 1477/81
Guillaume Jouvenel des Ursins, Chancellor of France, circa 1460
Wood   93 × 73.2 cm
Purchased in 1835

JEAN FOUQUET
Tours, *circa* 1420 – Tours, 1477/81
Charles VII, King of France, circa 1445(?)
Wood   85.7 × 70.6 cm
Purchased in 1838

JEAN HEY, called the Master of Moulins
Active in central France between 1480 and 1500
Charles-Orlant, Dauphin of France, 1494
Wood   28.5 × 23.5
Presented by Carlos de Beistegui, 1942

JEAN HEY, called the Master of Moulins
Active in central France between 1480
   and 1500
A donor and St. Mary Magdalen, circa 1490
Wood   56 × 40 cm
Purchased in 1904

FLEMISH ARTIST IN PARIS, mid–15th century
The Paris Parlement altar-piece, probably commissioned in 1452
Wood   226.5 × 270 cm
Seized during the French Revolution

Executed by a Flemish artist strongly influenced by the
work of Rogier van der Weyden, this altar-piece, still in its
original carved wood frame, shows the patrons of the
French monarchy (St. Louis, St. Denis, and Charlemagne)
grouped around the Crucifixion. In the background, on
the left-hand side, is a very accurate depiction of the
Louvre as it was in the middle of the fifteenth century.
Until the French Revolution the altar-piece hung in the
Chambre Dorée of the Paris Parlement and can be seen
there in Nicolas Lancret's painting of the Parlement
(see p. 61).

ENGUERRAND QUARTON
Active in Provence between 1444 and 1466
The Villeneuve-les-Avignon Pietà, circa 1455(?)
Wood   163 × 218.5 cm
Presented by the Société des Amis du Louvre, 1905

NICOLAS DIPRE
Active in Avignon from 1495 – Avignon, 1532
The Presentation of the Virgin, circa 1500
Wood   31.7 × 50 cm
Presented by Pierre Landry, 1972 ▶

One of the supreme examples of medieval painting, this
Pietà should now, after many years of discussion, be
recognised as a masterpiece by Quarton. The boldly
simplified and outlined forms, directness of treatment and
clarity of light are all characteristics of the School of
Provence in the fifteenth century. They are also found in
The Boulbon altar-piece and Dipre's *Presentation of the Virgin*;
and to a lesser extent in Lieferinxe's later *Crucifixion*.

PROVENÇAL ARTIST, mid–15th century
The Boulbon altar-piece, circa *1460*
Wood transferred to canvas   172 × 227.8 cm
Presented by the Committee for the exhibition of
    French primitive art, 1904

JOSSE LIEFERINXE, the Master of St. Sebastien
Hainaut, active in Provence from 1493 – Provence, 1505/08
The Crucifixion, circa 1500/05(?)
Wood   170 × 126 cm
Purchased in 1962

Attributed to Jean Clouet
?, 1485/90 – ?, 1540/41
François I, King of France, circa 1530(?)
Wood   96 × 74 cm
Collection of François I

Jean Cousin the Elder
Sens, *circa* 1490 – Paris, *circa* 1560
Eva Prima Pandora, circa 1550(?)
Wood   97.5 × 150 cm
Presented by the Société des Amis du Louvre, 1922

SCHOOL OF FONTAINEBLEAU, mid-16th century
Charity, circa 1560(?)
Canvas   147 × 96.5 cm
Purchased in 1970

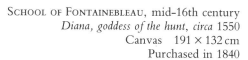

SCHOOL OF FONTAINEBLEAU, mid-16th century
Diana, goddess of the hunt, circa 1550
Canvas   191 × 132 cm
Purchased in 1840

JEAN DE GOURMONT
Carquebut, *circa* 1483 – ?, after 1551
The Adoration of the shepherds, circa 1525(?)
Wood   93.5 × 115.5 cm
From the chapel of the Château d'Écouen

The setting of dreamlike architecture in this picture, clearly
inspired by Roman antiquity, although it is difficult to tell
whether it is under construction or in ruins, is given far
more prominence than the religious subject-matter.
Gourmont, who worked first in Paris and then in Lyons,
also executed engravings in which he often exploited his
virtuoso study of perspective.

Françoise Clouet
? – Paris, 1572
Pierre Quthe, apothecary, 1562
Wood   91 × 70 cm
Presented by the Société des Amis du Louvre, 1908

FRANÇOIS CLOUET
? – Paris, 1572
Elisabeth of Austria, Queen of France, 1571(?)
Wood   36 × 26 cm
Collection of Louis XV; entered the Louvre in 1817

FRENCH ARTIST, second half of the 16th century
Portrait of a flautist with one eye, 1566
Wood   62 × 50 cm
Presented by Percy Moore Turner, 1948

CORNEILLE DE LYON
The Hague, *circa* 1500 – Lyons(?),
     circa 1575
Jean de Bourbon-Vendôme, circa 1550(?)
Wood   19 × 15.5 cm
Purchased in 1883

CORNEILLE DE LYON
The Hague, *circa* 1500 – Lyons(?),
     circa 1575
Pierre Aymeric, 1534
Wood   16.5 × 14.2 cm
Purchased in 1976

ANTOINE CARON
Beauvais, 1521 – Paris, 1599
Augustus and the Sybil, circa 1575/80
Canvas   125 × 170 cm
Presented by Gustave Lebel, 1938

Caron, who was Cathérine de Médicis' official artist and
whose paintings often seem to echo the royal fêtes, shows
here the Emperor Augustus on his knees in front of the
Sybil, who gestures towards the Virgin and Child in the
heavens. The architectural setting, reminiscent of theatre
decor, shows the Seine and possibly certain monuments of
Paris modified by the artist's imagination on the right-
hand side.

SCHOOL OF FONTAINEBLEAU, late 16th century
Gabrielle d'Estrées and one of her sisters, circa 1595(?)
Wood   96 × 125 cm
Purchased in 1937

TOUSSAINT DUBREUIL
Paris, *circa* 1561 – Paris, 1602
Subject-matter unknown, called *A pagan sacrifice,*
   circa 1600(?)
Canvas   190 × 140 cm
From the 'Château Neuf', Saint-Germain-en-Laye

FRENCH ARTIST, early 17th century
Portrait of a couple, circa 1610(?)
Wood   73 × 96 cm
Purchased in 1967

The seventeenth century

The history of the Louvre's collection of seventeenth-century paintings illustrates changes in taste and the ways in which the rich and complex period has been valued. The collection, formed gradually by different contributions, first reflects the predilections of kings and then those of art historians.

Louis XIII acquired few works and the ones he owned came from vast pictorial schemes: the three allegorical figures by Vouet (p. 34), formerly part of the decoration of the Château Neuf, Saint-Germain-en-Laye, and two large works by Poussin from his Parisian period, *The institution of the Eucharist* (p. 38) commissioned in 1640 and also from Saint-Germain, and the ceiling painting *Truth carried off by Time* bequeathed by Cardinal Richelieu to the King with the Palais Cardinal, now the Palais Royal.

It was Louis XIV who, with unprecedented largesse, formed a magnificent collection of French art, a group of paintings which was essentially 'classical' in taste; a taste which could even be called 'Roman'—powerful and masculine, contrasting and often epic. In fact the collection chiefly consisted of works by three artists who were Roman by adoption, Poussin, Claude and Valentin, the only paintings considered worthy of being hung next to Italian sixteenth- and seventeenth-century masters, and of course it included paintings by the King's official artists, Le Brun and later Mignard. Thirty-one of the thirty-eight Poussins in the Louvre, a collection unrivalled anywhere in the world, belonged to Louis XIV. In 1665 he bought the Duc de Richelieu's thirteen famous canvases, amongst them *The four seasons* (p. 38), *Diogenes*, *Eliezer and Rebecca*, *The plague at Ashdod* (p. 36) and *The rescue of Pyrrhus*. Seven others were acquired in 1685, and in 1693 Le Nôtre gave the King *The adulterous woman, St. John baptising the people* and *The rescue of the infant Moses by Pharaoh's daughter*. Of the Louvre's works by Claude, ten came from Louis XIV, some were bought from the Duc de Richelieu, while others were given by Le Nôtre. Nearly all the Le Bruns, except those seized from churches during the French Revolution, and nearly all the Mignards also came to the Louvre from the King's collection. However, the collection was not confined only to these artists; works by a variety of other artists also feature in the 1710 inventory, among them *Charity* by Blanchard, *Acis and Galatea* by Perrier, *Augustus at Alexander's tomb* by Bourdon, and three by Stella, including *The Virgin and St. Anne* (now in Rouen) and *Minerva and the Muses* (p. 41).

Louis XV bought paintings that showed him to be heir to his great-grandfather's taste for solemn and heroic works. He bought Poussin's enormous *St. Francis Xavier* at the Jesuits' sale when their order was suppressed in 1763. At the same time Jean de Jullienne bought Vouet's *The Presentation in the Temple* (p. 35) which he gave to the Académie and which later entered the Louvre with the Académie's collection. The King also bought two fine Valentins from the estate of the Prince de Carignan in 1742.

Louis XVI, however, appreciated another aspect of seventeenth-century art, one that had previously been ignored by royal collectors. Contrary to the 'Roman' taste of Louis XIV, he and his Surintendant des Bâtiments, the Comte d'Angiviller, had what one might call 'Parisian' taste. Poussin was still appreciated, but as the King already had his ancestor's collection he concentrated on acquiring these more 'Parisian' works which were restrained, delicate and refined, with a predominance of clear, soft colours, not unlike the first works by eighteenth-century neo-classical artists such as Lagrenée. An artist who now became very popular was Eustache Le Sueur. In 1776 two large cycles by him entered the royal collection: twenty-two paintings depicting the life of St. Bruno painted for Chartreuse in Paris were given to the King by the monks at the instigation of the Comte d'Angiviller; whilst the decorative series from the Hôtel Lambert on the Île Saint-Louis, one from the Chambre des Muses (p. 47) and the other from the Cabinet de l'Amour were also acquired at this time. Louis XVI also bought Le Sueur's fine group portrait known as *A gathering of friends* (p. 46) and *Laban searching Jacob's baggage for the stolen idols* by La Hyre (p. 40).

Many paintings of similar 'Parisian' taste entered the collection during the French Revolution. Several were seized from the nobility: two small canvases by La Hyre from the Comte d'Angiviller, from the Duc de Penthièvre and the Duc d'Orléans two distinct and elegant Bourdons, and from the Quentin-Crawford collection two rare works by Stella. Also during the Revolution, Poussin's *Camillus and the schoolmaster of Falerii* was seized with the rest of the collection from the Galerie Dorée in the Duc de Penthièvre's Hôtel de Toulouse, and two little works by Claude were taken from the Duc de Brissac. Seizures from convents and churches constituted a major contribution: an enormous number of paintings, often of vast proportions, were thus added to the national collection, including nearly all the works by Philippe de Champaigne now in the Louvre and many masterpieces by Le Sueur, Bourdon, Le Brun and La Hyre. Despite this great influx of riches, paintings continued to be purchased, the government of the Directory buying Poussin's *Self-portrait* (p. 36) in 1797.

Very few contributions were made during the first half of the nineteenth century. However, Champaigne's masterpiece, *Portrait of a man* (p. 42) was purchased by Vivant Denon, Director of the Museum, in 1806 and another portrait by Champaigne was bought in 1835, a double portrait reputedly of Mansart and Perrault. *Apollo and Daphne*, Poussin's last painting, left unfinished at his death, was bought during the Second Empire; but it was not until 1911 that *The inspiration of the poet* (p. 37) entered the Louvre.

With the progressive rediscovery of a seventeenth century which could be termed 'realist' during the last half of the nineteenth century and the beginning of the twentieth, a new visual awareness reinstated 'painters of reality'. The seventeenth-century art of the La Caze collection was realist: besides the two large state portraits by Champaigne and a *'bambochade'* by Bourdon, there was above all *The peasant's meal* by Le Nain. Between 1869 and 1915 seven paintings by the Le Nain brothers entered the Louvre, including *The haywain* (p. 44) and *The peasant family* (p. 43). It was during these same years that mid-nineteenth-century artists such as Courbet, Millet and Rousseau, expounders of another kind of realism, began at last to appear in the

Louvre's collection. Twentieth-century keepers, who have continued to augment the series by the Le Nain brothers, added still lifes, absent until then, such as those by Baugin and Dupuis (p. 45), and formed the finest collection of paintings by Georges de La Tour in existence, notably the famous *Christ with St. Joseph* (p. 32). Acquisitions began in 1926 and continued progressively as La Tour's work was rediscovered. Recently the Louvre has been enhanced by the addition of two more famous canvases by him, *The cheat* (p. 32) from the Landry collection and *St. Sebastian tended by Irene* (p. 33), presented by the Société des Amis du Louvre, as well as two masterpieces by the Le Nain brothers, the delightful *Victory* and *The group of smokers* traditionally known as *The guard-room* (p. 44). The moving portrait of *Arnauld d'Andilly* in old age, painted by Champaigne at the end of his life, entered the collection in 1979 in lieu of death duties, and in 1980 the Société des Amis du Louvre, ever generous, presented Bourdon's lyrical *A subject from Roman history* (p. 46), filling a gap in the collection.

The Louvre now possesses a superb collection of seventeeth-century French painting with all its different facets represented. This will become even more apparent when the huge works by Champaigne, Le Sueur, Le Brun and Poussin, which have been confined to the reserve collection for so long, are finally exhibited. However, even with such a magnificent display there are a few gaps to be filled. For instance, the Louvre has no late work by Claude nor a major painting by La Hyre. Except for Valentin, the French followers of Caravaggio are poorly represented, despite two important recent acquisitions, *The young singer* (p. 30), one of the most successful pictures executed by Vignon during his stay in Rome and the huge and somewhat unadventurous *Prince Marcantonio Doria* painted by Vouet in Genoa (p. 34). The century also produced a large number of highly successful still life painters, who are meagrely represented in the Louvre's collection. Today some of these are perhaps considered second-rate, but opinions are constantly changing. At the beginning of this century few people had heard of Georges de La Tour.

VALENTIN DE BOULOGNE
Coulommiers, 1594 – Rome, 1632
Concert with Roman bas-relief, circa 1622/25
Canvas   173 × 214 cm
Collection of Louis XV, purchased in 1742

VALENTIN DE BOULOGNE
Coulommiers, 1594 – Rome, 1632
The judgement of Solomon, circa 1625(?)
Canvas   176 × 210 cm
Collection of Louis XIV, purchased in 1661

The influence of Caravaggio's dramatic style which
revolutionised European painting at the beginning of the
seventeenth century can be seen clearly in Valentin's work.
He would have come into contact with Caravaggio's work
in Rome where he went as a very young man, and spent all
of his short career. In *The judgement of Solomon* the strength
of forms outlined against the shadow, so reminiscent of
Caravaggio, does not preclude an atmosphere of mystery
and poetry that is peculiar to Valentin. Louis XIV owned
several of his paintings; five are still hanging in the King's
bedchamber in the Château de Versailles.

CLAUDE VIGNON
Tours, 1593 – Paris, 1670
The young singer, circa 1622/23
Canvas   95 × 90 cm
Presented by the Société des Amis du Louvre,
  1966

VALENTIN DE BOULOGNE
Coulommiers, 1594 – Rome, 1632
The fortune-teller, circa 1628
Canvas   125 × 175 cm
Collection of Louis XIV, purchased before 1683

CLAUDE VIGNON
Tours, 1593 – Paris, 1670
Solomon and the Queen of Sheba, 1624
Canvas   80 × 119 cm
Purchased in 1933

NICOLAS RÉGNIER
Maubeuge, 1591 – Venice, 1667
The fortune-teller, circa 1625
Canvas   127 × 150 cm
Purchased in 1816

GEORGES DE LA TOUR
Vic-sur-Seille, 1593 – Lunéville, 1652
The cheat, circa 1635(?)
Canvas   106 × 146 cm
Purchased in 1972

GEORGES DE LA TOUR
Vic-sur-Seille, 1593 – Lunéville, 1652
Christ with St. Joseph in the carpenter's shop, circa 1640(?)
Canvas   137 × 102 cm
Presented by Percy Moore Turner, 1948

GEORGES DE LA TOUR
Vic-sur-Seille, 1593 – Lunéville, 1652
The penitent Magdalen with night-light, called
The Terff Magdalen, circa 1640/45(?)
Canvas   128 × 94 cm
Purchased in 1949

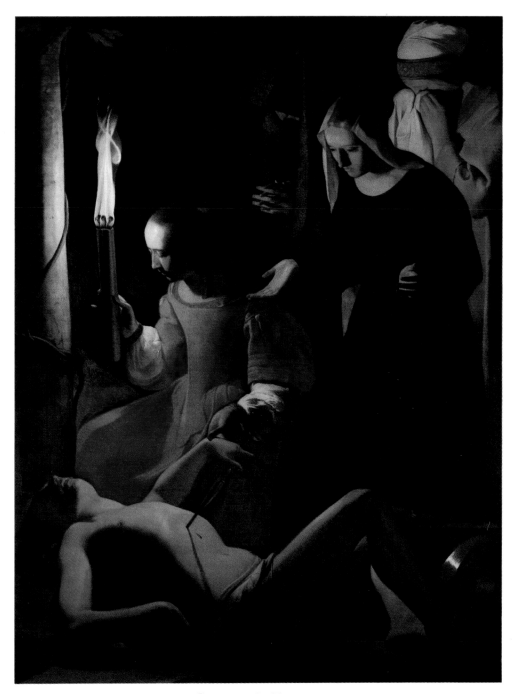

GEORGES DE LA TOUR
Vic–sur–Seille, 1593 – Lunéville, 1652
St. Sebastian tended by Irene, 1649(?)
Canvas   167 × 131 cm
Presented by the Société des Amis du Louvre, 1979

This painting was discovered in the church of Bois–
Anzeray in 1945 and is almost certainly the canvas known
to have been given by the town of Lunéville to La Ferté,
governor of Lorraine at the end of 1649. It is the most
complete and ambitious of La Tour's night scenes, with the
blue of the coat reverberating in the range of warm tones,
and is also one of his last works. An old copy of good
quality is in the museum of Berlin–Dahlem.

SIMON VOUET
Paris, 1590 – Paris, 1649
Prince Marcantonio Doria, 1621
Canvas   129 × 95 cm
Anonymous gift, 1979

SIMON VOUET
Paris, 1590 – Paris, 1649
Allegory of wealth, circa 1630/35
Canvas   170 × 124 cm
Collection of Louis XIII

NICOLAS TOURNIER
Montbéliard, 1590 – Toulouse(?), 1638/39
Crucifixion with the Virgin, St. John and St. Vincent de Paul, circa
    1635(?)
Canvas   422 × 292 cm
Exchanged with the Musée de Toulouse in 1800

SIMON VOUET
Paris, 1590 – Paris, 1649
The Presentation in the Temple, 1641
Canvas   393 × 250 cm
From the main altar of the Jesuit church
now Saint Paul-Saint Louis, Paris
Collection of the Académie

NICOLAS POUSSIN
Les Andelys, 1594 – Rome, 1665
Self-portrait, 1650
Canvas 98 × 74 cm
Purchased in 1797

NICOLAS POUSSIN
Les Andelys, 1594 – Rome, 1665
The plague at Ashdod, 1630
Canvas 148 × 198 cm
Collection of Louis XIV, purchased in 1665

NICOLAS POUSSIN
Les Andelys, 1594 – Rome, 1665
Echo and Narcissus, circa 1628/30(?)
Canvas 74 × 100 cm
Collection of Louis XIV, purchased
before 1683

NICOLAS POUSSIN
Les Andelys, 1594 – Rome, 1665
The inspiration of the poet, *circa* 1630(?)
Canvas   182.5 × 213 cm
Purchased in 1911

Poussin spent almost all his career in Rome painting in isolation. He endeavoured to create a clear visual language that would appeal to the spectator's mind and affect him rationally rather than through the emotions. His oeuvre is one of the supreme expressions of classicism in French art. The subject of *The inspiration of the poet* remains under discussion: it is possible that the young man on the right, being inspired by Apollo, is Virgil and the figure standing on the left Calliope, muse of epic poetry. In both figures there are direct references to antique sculpture, as so often in Poussin's work, and the golden light shows the influence of the great Venetian painters of the sixteenth century.

NICOLAS POUSSIN
Les Andelys, 1594 – Rome, 1665
The institution of the Eucharist, 1640
Canvas   325 × 250 cm
Painted for the Sainte-Chapelle,
    Saint-Germain-en-Laye
Collection of Louis XIII

NICOLAS POUSSIN
Les Andelys, 1594 – Rome, 1665
Winter or *The Deluge*, between 1660 and
    1664
Canvas   118 × 160 cm
One of a series of four paintings
    depicting the seasons
Collection of Louis XIV, purchased in
    1665

Claude Gellée, called Le Lorrain
Chamagne, 1600 – Rome, 1682
The disembarkation of Cleopatra at Tarsus, circa
  1642/43
Canvas   119 × 170 cm
Collection of Louis XIV, purchased before 1683

Claude Gellée, called Le Lorrain
Chamagne, 1600 – Rome, 1682
Ulysses returns Chryseis to her father, 1648(?)
Canvas   119 × 150 cm
Collection of Louis XIV, purchased in 1665

Claude Gellée, called Le Lorrain
Chamagne, 1600 – Rome, 1682
Landscape with Paris and Oenone, called *The ford*,
  1648
Canvas   119 × 150 cm
This painting is a pendant to *Ulysses returns*
  Chryseis to her father above
Collection Louis XIV, purchased in 1665

JACQUES BLANCHARD
Paris, 1600 – Paris, 1638
Venus and the three Graces surprised by a
*   mortal, circa* 1631/33
Canvas   170 × 218 cm
Purchased in 1921

LAURENT DE LA HYRE
Paris, 1606 – Paris(?), 1656
Laban searching Jacob's baggage for the stolen idols, 1647
Canvas   95 × 133 cm
Collection of Louis XVI

FRANÇOIS PERRIER
Saint-Jean-de-Losne (?), *circa* 1600(?) –
    Paris, 1650
Aeneas and his companions fighting the
*   Harpies, circa* 1646/47
Canvas   155 × 218 cm
From the Cabinet de l'Amour in the
    Hôtel Lambert, Paris
Collection of Louis XVI, purchased in
    1776

PIERRE PATEL the Elder
Picardy, *circa* 1605 – Paris, 1676
Landscape with ruins, circa 1646/47
Canvas   73 × 150 cm
From the Cabinet de l'Amour in the
   Hôtel Lambert, Paris.
Collection of Louis XVI, purchased in
   1776

JACQUES STELLA
Lyons, 1596 – Paris, 1657
Minerva and the Muses, circa 1640/50
Canvas   116 × 162 cm
Collection of Louis XIV

PHILIPPE DE CHAMPAIGNE
Brussels, 1602 – Paris, 1674
The miracles of the penitent St. Mary, 1656
Canvas   219 × 336 cm
From the apartments of Anne of Austria in the convent
   of Val de Grâce, Paris
Seized during the French Revolution

PHILIPPE DE CHAMPAIGNE
Brussels, 1602 – Paris, 1674
Portrait of a man, 1650
Canvas 91 × 72 cm
Purchased in 1906

PHILIPPE DE CHAMPAIGNE
Brussels, 1602 – Paris, 1674
The Ex-voto of 1662, 1662
Canvas 165 × 229 cm
Seized during the French Revolution

LOUIS or ANTOINE LE NAIN
Laon, *circa* 1600/10 – Paris, 1648
The peasant family, *circa* 1640/45
Canvas   113 × 159 cm
Purchased in 1915

The peasant family is the most monumental and moving of
the peasant subject paintings for which the Le Nain
brothers are renowned. There was no equivalent in
seventeenth-century European painting and the low-keyed
tones and careful attention given to the individuals were
not to be seen again until the nineteenth century in the
work of Realists such as Corot or Millet.

LOUIS or ANTOINE LE NAIN
Laon, *circa* 1600/10 – Paris, 1648
The haywain, also called *The return from hay-making*, 1641
Canvas   56 × 76 cm
Bequeathed by Vicomte Philippe de Saint-Albin, 1879

LOUIS or ANTOINE LE NAIN
Laon, *circa* 1600/10 – Paris, 1648
The group of smokers, also called *The guard-room*, 1643
Canvas   117 × 137 cm
Purchased in 1969

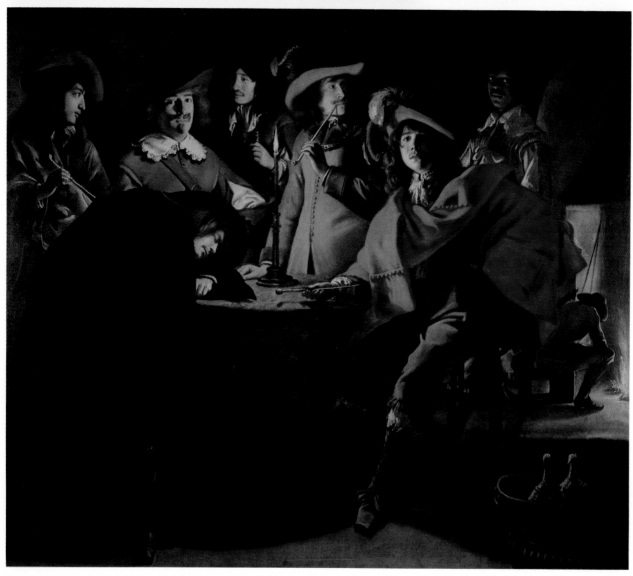

MATHIEU (?) LE NAIN
Laon, *circa* 1608/10 – Paris, 1677
The supper at Emmaus, circa 1645(?)
Canvas   75 × 92 cm
Purchased in 1950

LUBIN BAUGIN
Pithiviers, *circa* 1612 – Paris, 1663
Still life with wafer biscuits, circa 1630/35
Wood   41 × 52 cm
Purchased in 1954

PIERRE DUPUIS
Monfort l'Amaury, 1610 – Paris, 1682
Still life with basket of grapes, circa 1650(?)
Canvas   50 × 60 cm
Purchased in 1951

SÉBASTIEN BOURDON
Montpellier, 1616 – Paris, 1671
The beggars, circa 1635/40(?)
Wood   49 × 65 cm
Royal Collection

Sébastien Bourdon
Montpellier, 1616 – Paris, 1671
A scene from Roman history (*Antony and Cleopatra?*), *circa* 1645(?)
Canvas   145 × 197 cm
Presented by the Société des Amis du Louvre, 1979

Eustache Le Sueur
Paris, 1617 – Paris, 1655
Group portrait, called *A gathering of friends*, *circa* 1640/42
Canvas   127 × 195 cm
Collection of Louis XVI

EUSTACHE LE SUEUR
Paris, 1617 – Paris, 1655
Three muses: Melpomene, Erato and Polyhymnia,
circa 1652/55
Wood 130 × 130 cm
From the Chambre des Muses in the Hôtel
Lambert, Paris
Collection of Louis XVI, purchased in 1776

EUSTACHE LE SUEUR
Paris, 1617 – Paris, 1655
St. Gervase and St. Protase brought before Anastasius
for refusing to sacrifice to Jupiter, commissioned in
1652
Canvas 357 × 684 cm
Cartoon for the tapestry in Saint Gervais, Paris
Seized during the French Revolution

CHARLES LE BRUN
Paris, 1619 – Paris, 1690
Pietà, between 1643/45
Canvas   146 × 222 cm
Seized during the French Revolution

CHARLES LE BRUN
Paris, 1619 – Paris, 1690
Alexander and Porus, exhibited at the
    Salon of 1673
Canvas   470 × 1264 cm
Collection of Louis XIV

CHARLES LE BRUN
Paris, 1619 – Paris, 1690
Chancellor Séguier, circa 1655/57
Canvas   295 × 351 cm
Purchased in 1942, with the help of the
Société des Amis du Louvre

CHARLES LE BRUN
Paris, 1619 – Paris, 1690
The Adoration of the shepherds, 1689
Canvas   151 × 213 cm
Collection of Louis XIV

PIERRE MIGNARD
Troyes, 1612 – Paris, 1695
The Virgin of the grapes, circa 1640/50(?)
Canvas   121 × 94 cm
Collection of Louis XIV

The end of Louis XIV's reign and the Regency

It could seem somewhat arbitrary to group together artists from the end of Louis XIV's reign and those from his nephew's Regency. Rigaud's *Louis XIV* (p. 55) and Watteau's *Pilgrimage to Cythera* (p. 59) each seem to typify the mood of the century in which they were produced; the first by its ostentation and solemnity, the second by its refined and dreamy elegance, although only sixteen years separate them. For a long time French painting of around 1700 was deemed to be uninteresting, academic and too much influenced by the taste of the court. Now, after recent art historical research, and new evaluation of the work of Rubens and Titian, the variety and creativity of this period are appreciated, and it is interesting, despite the difference in generations, to consider La Fosse, Jouvenet, Coypel, Rigaud and Largillière with the younger Watteau and Lemoyne (both of whom died young), since all acknowledge their debt to the rich and supple execution of Flemish painters and the delightful colour ranges used by the Venetians.

Most of the decorative works commissioned by Louis XIV still adorn, or have now been returned to, the palaces for which they were executed but some works by Coypel, La Fosse and Desportes from the royal collection are now in the Louvre. Paintings depicting the King's victories by Van der Meulen (p. 53) or Parrocel (p. 53) were also part of the royal collection and are now in the Louvre, as is the portrait of the King by Rigaud, a symbol of the French monarchy. The canvas had been intended as a gift for Philip V of Spain, Louis XIV's grandson, but on seeing the painting the King liked it so much that he decided to keep it and had a replica made to send to Madrid. During Louis XV's reign the collection acquired other paintings, for example, Rigaud bequeathed his last work, *The Presentation in the Temple* (p. 56), which owes so much to Rembrandt, to the King. Louis XVI still bought Coypels, Van der Meulens and he bought one canvas by Louis de Boulogne. But by then the taste for works of Louis XIV's period and that of the Regency was out of fashion and it was not until the Revolution that new paintings came into the collection: three little works by Lemoyne seized from the nobility and above all the fine series of Jouvenet's work from Parisian churches. During the Restoration Rigaud's portrait of *Bossuet* and Jouvenet's portrait of *Dr. Raymond Finot* (p. 55) were purchased, the latter because it was thought to be of Fagon, Louis XIV's doctor.

With the Académie collection, which entered the Louvre during the Revolution, came a number of Académie election paintings, many of which are masterpieces: Rigaud's portrait of *Desjardins* executed in 1692 for his acceptance in 1700, Largillière's portrait of *Le Brun* (1686), Desportes' *Self portrait as a huntsman* (1699) (p. 57), Santerre's *Susanna bathing* and Pater's *Fête champêtre* (1728). But the most important of these was the *Pilgrimage to Cythera* (p. 59), Watteau's most popular painting and for a long time the only one by him in the Louvre. In the Académie's collection were other important paintings such as Rigaud's *Portrait of the artist's mother from two different angles* (p. 55) bequeathed to the Académie by the painter, and Jouvenet's *The Descent from the Cross* (p. 54).

Of very great importance to the Louvre was the bequest of the La Caze collection in 1869. Dr. Louis La Caze, a painter himself, was a keen collector of well-executed pictures with vigorous brushwork, and therefore favoured works from a period influenced by Titian, Rubens and Rembrandt. His taste can be seen in the *Democritus* by Antoine Coypel (p. 57) and in *Hercules and Omphale* by Lemoyne (p. 62). The breadth and quality of collections of works by certain artists in the Louvre is entirely due to the generosity of La Caze. For example, he bequeathed six works by Largillière, including the *Family portrait* (p. 57) originally thought to be of the artist himself and his family, and many works by Pater and Watteau. La Caze's eight Watteaus, including *The judgement of Paris* (p. 58) and *Gilles* (p. 60), which had belonged to Vivant Denon, Director of the Musée Napoléon, meant that this most poetic of French painters was at last fairly well represented in the Louvre.

Since then acquisitions of paintings from this period have been rare: a few works by Largillière have been given or bequeathed, a couple of theatre subjects by Gillot purchased in 1923 (p. 58) and in 1945, two rare silvery Lancrets, *The seat of justice* (p. 61) and *The decoration of the order of the Holy Spirit* were purchased in 1949, and a small Watteau landscape was presented in 1937. Recently two unusual works by Largillière have been acquired, a small landscape in 1971 and, in 1979, the theatrical *Decorative composition* (p. 56). But most importantly the group of Watteaus, despite La Caze, is still rather meagre, but has been augmented by the *Portrait of a gentleman* (p. 58) and *Diana bathing*.

Not until the opening of the new rooms will the true extent of the Louvre's rich collection of paintings from this period be appreciated. The huge, glowing religious compositions by Jouvenet, particularly *The miraculous draught of fishes* and *The resurrection of Lazarus* painted for Saint-Nicolas-des-Champs in Paris, will reveal an aspect of painting during Watteau's time that is not as yet well enough known.

CHARLES DE LA FOSSE
Paris, 1636 – Paris, 1716
The rescue of the infant Moses by Pharaoh's daughter,
commissioned in 1701
Canvas 125 × 110 cm
Collection of Louis XIV

ADAM FRANS VAN DER MEULEN
Brussels, 1632 – Paris, 1690
The defeat of the Spanish army near Bruges canal, 1667,
circa 1670(?)
Canvas 50 × 80 cm
Collection of Louis XIV

JOSEPH PARROCEL
Brignoles, 1646 – Paris, 1704
The crossing of the Rhine by the army of
Louis XIV, 1672, 1699
Canvas 234 × 164 cm
Collection of Louis XIV

JEAN JOUVENET
Rouen, 1644 – Paris, 1717
The Descent from the Cross, 1697
Canvas   424 × 312 cm
Collection of the Académie

This bold and vigorous painting, with its magnificent
harmony of warm colours, foreshadows the most beautiful
of the nineteenth-century Romantic paintings. Executed
for the church of the Capuchins in the Place Louis-le-
grand, Paris, it was donated to the Académie Royale de
Peinture et de Sculpture in 1756. During the French
Revolution it was acquired by the Louvre, as were all the
other paintings which had belonged to the Académie.

HYACINTHE RIGAUD
Perpignan, 1659 – Paris, 1743
Portrait of the artist's mother from two different angles, 1695
Canvas   83 × 103 cm
Collection of the Académie

JEAN JOUVENET
Rouen, 1644 – Paris, 1717
Dr. Raymond Finot, exhibited at the
    Salon of 1704
Canvas   73 × 59 cm
Purchased in 1838

HYACINTHE RIGAUD
Perpignan, 1659 – Paris, 1743
Louis XIV, King of France, 1701
Canvas   277 × 194 cm
Collection of Louis XIV

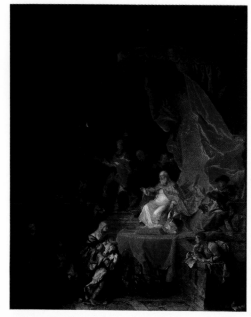

ANTOINE COYPEL
Paris, 1661 – Paris, 1722
The swooning of Esther, exhibited at the Salon of 1704
Canvas   105 × 137 cm
Collection of Louis XIV

HYACINTHE RIGAUD
Perpignan, 1659 – Paris, 1743
The Presentation in the Temple, 1743
Wood   83 × 68 cm
Collection of Louis XV

NICOLAS DE LARGILLIÈRE
Paris, 1656 – Paris, 1746
Decorative composition, circa 1720/30(?)
Canvas   261 × 253 cm
Purchased in 1979

ANTOINE COYPEL
Paris, 1661 – Paris, 1722
Democritus, 1692
Canvas 69 × 57 cm
Bequeathed by Louis La Caze, 1869

NICOLAS DE LARGILLIÈRE
Paris, 1656 – Paris, 1746
Family portrait, circa 1710(?)
Canvas 149 × 200 cm
Bequeathed by Louis La Caze, 1869

JEAN-BAPTISTE SANTERRE
Magny-en-Vexin, 1658 – Paris, 1717
Susanna bathing, 1704
Canvas 205 × 145 cm
Collection of the Académie

FRANÇOIS DESPORTES
Champigneulles, 1661 – Paris, 1743
Self-portrait as a huntsman, 1699
Canvas 197 × 163 cm
Collection of the Académie

CLAUDE GILLOT
Langres, 1673 – Paris, 1722
The two coaches, circa 1710(?)
Canvas   127 × 160 cm
Purchased in 1923

JEAN ANTOINE WATTEAU
Valenciennes, 1684 – Nogent-sur-Marne, 1721
Portrait of a gentleman, circa 1715/20
Canvas   130 × 97 cm
Purchased in 1973

JEAN ANTOINE WATTEAU
Valenciennes, 1684 – Nogent-sur
    Marne, 1721
The judgement of Paris, circa 1720(?)
Wood   47 × 31 cm
Bequeathed by Louis La Caze, 1869

JEAN ANTOINE WATTEAU
Valenciennes, 1684 – Nogent-sur-Marne, 1721
The pilgrimage to Cythera, 1717
Canvas   129 × 194 cm
Collection of the Académie

It was with this painting, called at that time *The pilgrimage to Cythera*, that Watteau was officially accepted by the Académie Royale de Peinture et de Sculpture in 1717. The title *The departure for Cythera* under which it became famous is in fact incorrect as the pilgrims are already on the Island of Venus and are preparing to leave. The subject was inspired by Rubens' *Garden of love*. The open, curving composition, the clear colours and general mood of both happiness and nostalgia, were to be important influences on French eighteenth-century painting.

JEAN ANTOINE WATTEAU
Valenciennes, 1684 – Nogent-sur-Marne, 1721
Gilles, circa 1718/20(?)
Canvas   184.5 × 149.5 cm
Bequeathed by Louis La Caze, 1869

FRANÇOIS LEMOYNE
Paris, 1688 – Paris, 1737
The Assumption of the Virgin, circa 1731
Canvas   91.5 × 119 cm
Purchased in 1924

NICOLAS LANCRET
Paris, 1690 – Paris, 1743
*The seat of justice in the Parlement of
 Paris (1723), circa* 1724(?)
Canvas   56 × 81.5 cm
Purchased in 1949

JEAN-BAPTISTE PATER
Valenciennes, 1695 – Paris, 1736
The Chinese hunt, 1736
Canvas   55 × 46 cm
Presented by the Office des Biens Privés, 1950

FRANÇOIS LEMOYNE
Paris, 1688 – Paris, 1737
Hercules and Omphale, 1724
Canvas   184 × 149 cm
Bequeathed by Louis La Caze, 1869

The mid-eighteenth century

It is disappointing that Louis XV was not a keen collector, for during his reign sovereigns from the rest of Europe were voraciously buying contemporary French paintings: Frederick II of Prussia acquired the Watteaus, Lancrets and Chardins which today are the glory of Charlottenburg; his sister Louise-Ulrique of Sweden, well advised by her French ambassador Tessin, purchased the finest Bouchers and Chardins; Catherine the Great, Empress of Russia, bought the entire collection belonging to Louis-Antoine Crozat, Baron de Thiers, after his death in 1770. Comprising important paintings from all periods, the Crozat collection also included contemporary works. Louis XV, on the other hand, did not own a single painting by Watteau or Fragonard. He did, however, commission a number of paintings to hang over doors: still lifes from Chardin, such as the *Attributes of the Arts* and the *Attributes of Music* for the Château de Choisy, and from Lancret *The four seasons* for the Château de la Muette. For the Château de Fontainebleau he commissioned Van Loo's *The halt during the hunt* (p. 69) and Parrocel's *The halt of the grenadiers*. Many of the Bouchers, and the only Fragonard, *Chaereas and Callirrhoe* (p. 81), purchased during Louis XV's reign were tapestry cartoons and not easel paintings. Nevertheless, he did buy two of Chardin's most beautiful works at the Salon of 1740, *The diligent mother* (p. 72) and *Saying grace*. Also, the Marquis de Marigny, Surintendant des Bâtiments from 1751 to 1774, commissioned some large series which cannot be overlooked. One example of these is the group of fifteen large paintings depicting *The ports of France*, commissioned from Joseph Vernet in 1753 and completed in 1765. Today, except for the two in the Louvre (p. 78), this series is in the Musée de la Marine.

Louis XVI seems to have been scarcely more fond of contemporary painting than his grandfather but did purchase works by Subleyras, Carle Van Loo and Raoux, the most refined and restrained of eighteenth-century artists. He bought Greuze's already popular *The village bride* (p. 78) in 1782 at the sale following the death of the Marquis de Marigny, and commissioned Hubert Robert to paint the four large *Antiquities of France* (p. 84) for the Château de Fontainebleau.

Among works seized during the Revolution were six paintings by Subleyras from the Comte d'Angiviller, the Comte de Pestre Senef and the Duc de Penthièvre among others; and several landscapes by Joseph Vernet from the Comtesse du Barry, the Duchesse de Noailles and Boutin, Treasurer of the Navy. Two works by Vien and *The broken jug* by Greuze, one of his sentimental works which was highly regarded at the time, were also seized from the Comtesse du Barry. The Académie collection contained many important canvases of this period: election pieces by Boucher, *Renaud and Armide* (1734), Chardin, *The skate* and *The buffet* (p. 73), Tocqué, portraits of *Galloche* and *Lemoyne* (1734); portraits of *Oudry* and *Adam* (1753) by Perronneau and *Septimus Severus* (1769) by Greuze. Many works by Restout were taken from the churches and convents in Paris. A rare example of a French painting 'captured' abroad and subsequently left in the Louvre was Subleyras' vast *Christ in the house of Simon* which came from the convent of Asti near Turin to join the sketch for it which had been acquired by Louis XVI twelve years earlier. Subleyras (once again a 'Roman'), author of austere but delicate works, was one of the only painters from the first half of the eighteenth century to be appreciated during the neo-classical period (pp. 70 and 71). Not until the mid-nineteenth century was much interest taken in artists of Louis XV's reign, their work being considered frivolous and dissolute. Greuze, one aspect of whose work was serious and much concerned with virtue, was not scorned in quite the same way and the pair that complete *The father's curse, The ungrateful son* and *The punished son* (p. 79), were purchased in 1820.

The gift of Fragonard's *Music Lesson* in 1849 heralds a change in taste; *The inquisitive girls* by the same artist formed part of the Sauvageot gift in 1856. Chardin was now particularly appreciated and seven of his works were bought during the Second Empire, before the La Caze bequest, which was to form the major part of the Louvre's collection of mid-eighteenth-century French painting. With this bequest came the paintings that Louis XV and Louis XVI had not appreciated: thirteen major works by Chardin including *Still life with jar of olives* (p. 74), *The copper drinking fountain* (p. 74) and *The silver goblet*; nine sparkling Fragonards, among them *The bathers* (p. 83) and four imaginary figures; four Bouchers and several paintings by De Troy, Tocqué, Hubert Robert, Raoux, Nattier and Greuze. These beautiful works, which quickly became favourites with the public, were largely responsible for the general impression that the eighteenth century produced only small and charming paintings. La Caze's taste for these vigorous seductive works, canvases executed for collectors and avidly bought by them, even today tends to divert us from fully understanding the eighteenth century's ambitions towards '*la grande peinture*', paintings depicting subjects of morality and history.

The Louvre's collection continued to grow with purchases and bequests following on La Caze. Chardin's portraits of the Godefroy children, *Child with a top* and *Young man with a violin*, were purchased in 1907 and soon became popular; Boucher's *The afternoon meal* (p. 68) and the Louvre's most beautiful Nattier, *Comtesse Tessin* (p. 77), were bequeathed in 1895 by Dr. Achille Malécot; Chardin's *Portrait of Aved* (p. 72) was bequeathed by Paul Bureau in 1915; and several Greuzes were bequeathed by Baronne Nathaniel and Baron Arthur de Rothschild in 1899 and 1904. The bequest in 1915 of Baron Basile de Schlichting included works by Fragonard, Greuze, Nattier and Drouais.

Among more recent acquisitions the Carlos de Beistegui gift in 1942 contributed some important paintings: Fragonard's *Nude with cherubs* and an *Imaginary figure*; the most refined of Drouais, *Madame Drouais, wife of the artist* (p. 77); and a large work by Nattier, *The Duchesse de Chaulnes as Hébé*. The Sommier gift included Chardin's marvellous white and turquoise *The young draughtsman sharpening his pencil* (p. 75), the Péreire gift contained one of Vernet's most beautiful Italian scenes, *View of Naples*, which was later joined by its pair, another view of the same subject, and the Lyon gift (1961) contributed, amongst others, canvases by Robert and Vernet.

The most notable among recent acquisitions is the purchase of the famous *The bolt* (p. 83) one of the key pictures in Fragonard's late work.

More modest but nevertheless of great value are Subleyras' portrait of *Don Cesare Benvenuti* (p. 71), Delaporte's *Still life with a carafe of barley wine* (p. 74), and a youthful sketch by Boucher, which was bought in 1977, *Rebecca receiving Abraham's presents*. Among generous gifts should be mentioned the portrait of *Philippe Coypel* by his brother, Charles Antoine Coypel (p. 77) (Cailleux gift, 1968); Barbault's *The priest* and *The sultan* (François Heim gift, 1971); Dandré-Bardon's *Birth* (Benito Pardo gift, 1972); and Fragonard's *White bull* (Elaine and Michel David-Weill gift, 1976).

Thanks to the law which has been passed recently allowing the presentation of works of art in lieu of death duties, the Louvre's collection has gained three works which typify eighteenth-century France: Fragonard's portraits of the philosopher, *Diderot* (received in 1974) and the famous dancer, *Marie-Madeleine Guimard* (p. 82), and Chardin's *Still life with dead hare* (received in 1979). The policy of collecting views of the Louvre, which was originated by Hubert Robert, Director in the eighteenth century, should be mentioned. One painting was given by Maurice Fenaille in 1912, ten others have been purchased or given since 1946—interior and exterior, real and imaginary. The highlight of this project came in 1975 with the purchase of two large paintings that had been exhibited at the Salon of 1796, *Project for the redecoration of the Grande Galerie* and *Imaginary view of the Grande Galerie in ruins* (p. 84), both of which had for many years been in the Russian imperial collection in the palace of Tsarskoe-Selo.

Although pastels are not part of the collection of paintings in the Louvre but belong to the Department of Drawings, they should be mentioned because of their importance in French pictorial art as portraits 'painted in pastel'. The Louvre collection, unique both in number and quality, comes from the royal collection, the Académie collection and purchases and gifts during the nineteenth and twentieth centuries. The collections of works by Quentin de La Tour, Perronneau and Chardin, especially, are without equal.

Despite the fact that the Louvre's collection of paintings from the mid-eighteenth century rightly enjoys great prestige, there are nevertheless gaps that need to be filled. Few preliminary sketches, for example, which are one of the most attractive features of this period, have been acquired. However, it is important that, like that of the seventeenth century, eighteenth-century painting should be represented in all its different facets. The exhibition of the large canvases is a necessity which, with the opening of the new galleries in the Cour Carrée, will soon be realised. Only since 1968 has Fragonard's *Chaereas and Callirrhoe* been on view. At the beginning of this century one could see nearly all the French eighteenth-century paintings, small, medium or large, hung on thick material on three levels, frame touching frame, in the vast galleries which now display nineteenth-century art. Today such over-crowding would not be tolerated, but it is the Louvre's duty once again to exhibit the most important of the large paintings. Our entire vision of mid-eighteenth-century art could thus be changed.

Françoise Boucher
Paris, 1703 – Paris, 1770
Vulcan presenting Venus with arms for Aeneas, 1757
Canvas   320 × 320 cm
Tapestry cartoon for the Gobelins factory
Collection of Louis XV

This subject was often treated by Boucher, and the Louvre
has three other versions. The delightful and decorative
design, full of light and charm, was woven for the series of
tapestries *The loves of the gods*, and typifies the spirit of
Rococo decoration.

FRANÇOIS BOUCHER
Paris, 1703 – Paris, 1770
Diana bathing, 1742
Canvas   56 × 73 cm
Purchased in 1852

FRANÇOIS BOUCHER
Paris, 1703 – Paris, 1770
The forest, 1740
Canvas   131 × 163 cm
Presented by the Office des Biens
   Privés, 1951

FRANÇOIS BOUCHER
Paris, 1703 – Paris, 1770
The afternoon meal, 1739
Canvas   81.5 × 65.5 cm
Bequeathed by Dr. Achille Malécot, 1895

CARLE VAN LOO
Nice, 1705 – Paris, 1765
Aeneas carrying Anchises, 1729
Canvas   110 × 105 cm
Collection of Louis XVI

CARLE VAN LOO
Nice, 1705 – Paris, 1765
The halt during the hunt, 1737
Canvas   220 × 250 cm
Collection of Louis XV

JEAN-BAPTISTE OUDRY
Paris, 1686 – Beauvais, 1755
Still life with pheasant, 1753
Canvas   97 × 64 cm
Presented by the Office des Biens Privés, 1950

PIERRE SUBLEYRAS
Saint-Gilles-du-Gard, 1699 – Rome, 1749
Charon ferrying the Shades, circa 1735/40(?)
Canvas   135 × 83 cm
Seized during the French Revolution from the
collection of the Duc de Penthièvre

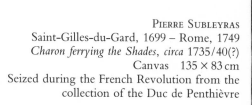

PIERRE SUBLEYRAS
Saint-Gilles-du-Gard, 1699 – Rome, 1749
Don Cesare Benvenuti , 1742
Canvas   138 × 101 cm
Purchased in 1969

JEAN SIMÉON CHARDIN
Paris, 1699 – Paris, 1779
Portrait of the artist Jacques André Joseph Aved, 1734
Canvas   138 × 105
Bequeathed by Paul Bureau, 1915

JEAN SIMÉON CHARDIN
Paris, 1699 – Paris, 1779
The diligent mother, exhibited at the Salon of 1740
Canvas   49 × 39 cm
Collection of Louis XV

It is said that Chardin began to paint interior scenes like *The diligent mother* because he was annoyed by someone saying that it was easy to paint still lifes. He based his art on the Dutch tradition, revolutionising it completely by his observation of reality and keen appreciation of colour tones.

Jean Siméon Chardin
Paris, 1699 – Paris, 1779
The buffet, 1728
Canvas   194 × 129 cm
Collection of the Académie

JEAN SIMÉON CHARDIN
Paris, 1699 – Paris, 1779
The copper drinking fountain, circa 1734
Wood   28.5 × 23 cm
Bequeathed by Louis La Caze, 1869

ROLAND DELAPORTE
Paris, 1724 – Paris, 1793
Still life with a carafe of barley wine, called '*La petite collation*', 1787
Canvas   37.5 × 46 cm
Purchased in 1979

JEAN SIMÉON CHARDIN
Paris, 1699 – Paris, 1779
Still life with jar of olives, 1760
Canvas   71 × 98 cm
Bequeathed by Louis La Caze, 1869

JEAN SIMÉON CHARDIN
Paris, 1699 – Paris, 1779
The young draughtsman sharpening his pencil, 1737
Canvas   80 × 65 cm
Presented by Madame Edmé Sommier, 1943

JEAN-BAPTISTE PERRONNEAU
Paris, 1715 – Amsterdam, 1783
Madame de Sorquainville, 1749
Canvas   101 × 81 cm
Presented by D. David Weill, 1937

FRANÇOIS-HUBERT DROUAIS
Paris, 1727 – Paris, 1775
Madame Drouais, wife of the artist,
circa 1758
Canvas   82.5 × 62 cm
Bequeathed by Carlos de
Beistegui, 1942

JEAN-MARC NATTIER
Paris, 1685 – Paris, 1766
Comtesse Tessin, 1741
Canvas   81 × 65 cm
Bequeathed by Dr. Achille Malécot,
1895

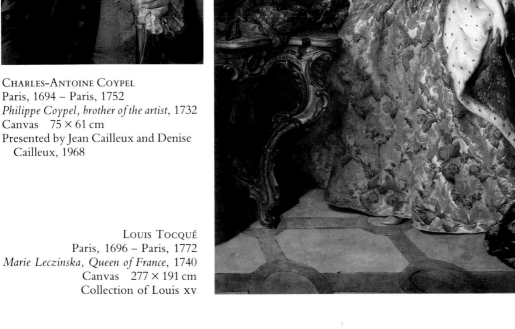

CHARLES-ANTOINE COYPEL
Paris, 1694 – Paris, 1752
Philippe Coypel, brother of the artist, 1732
Canvas   75 × 61 cm
Presented by Jean Cailleux and Denise
Cailleux, 1968

LOUIS TOCQUÉ
Paris, 1696 – Paris, 1772
Marie Leczinska, Queen of France, 1740
Canvas   277 × 191 cm
Collection of Louis XV

JOSEPH VERNET
Avignon, 1714 – Paris, 1789
View of Naples, 1748
Canvas   100 × 198 cm
Presented by André Péreire, 1949

JOSEPH VERNET
Avignon, 1714 – Paris, 1789
The town and harbour of Toulon, 1756
Canvas   165 × 263 cm
Collection of Louis XV

JEAN-BAPTISTE GREUZE
Tournus, 1725 – Paris, 1805
The village bride, exhibited at the Salon of 1761
Canvas   92 × 117 cm
Collection of Louis XVI, purchased in 1782

JEAN-BAPTISTE GREUZE
Tournus, 1725 – Paris, 1805
Self-portrait, circa 1785
Canvas   73 × 59 cm
Purchased in 1820

JEAN-BAPTISTE GREUZE
Tournus, 1725 – Paris, 1805
The punished son, 1778
Canvas   130 × 163 cm
Purchased in 1820

JOSEPH SIFFRED DUPLESSIS
Carpentras, 1725 – Versailles, 1802
Christophe Gabriel Allegrain, sculptor,
   1774
Canvas   130 × 97 cm
Collection of the Académie

NICOLAS BERNARD LÉPICIÉ
Paris, 1735 – Paris, 1784
The young draughtsman, Carle Vernet,
   aged fourteen, 1772
Canvas   41 × 33 cm
Bequeathed by Horace Paul Delaroche,
   1890

JEAN HONORÉ FRAGONARD
Grasse, 1732 – Paris, 1806
The storm, 1759(?)
Canvas   73 × 97 cm
Bequeathed by Louis La Caze, 1869

JEAN HONORÉ FRAGONARD
Grasse, 1732 – Paris, 1806
The high priest Chaereas sacrificing himself for Callirrhoe, 1765
Canvas   309 × 400 cm
Tapestry cartoon for the Gobelins factory (never executed)
Collection of Louis XV

It was thanks to this painting that Fragonard was accepted
by the Académie as a 'history painter'. He was soon to
abandon this type of subject–matter and devote himself to
the pleasant, often frivolous, paintings for which he is
famous. The movement in the composition, the sense of
drama and the strong light effects seen here are all in the
best tradition of Italian Baroque painting.

JEAN HONORÉ FRAGONARD
Grasse, 1732 – Paris, 1806
Mariê-Madeleine Guimard, dancer, circa 1769
Canvas 81.5 × 65 cm
Presented in lieu of death duties, 1974

JEAN HONORÉ FRAGONARD
Grasse, 1732 – Paris, 1806
The bathers, circa 1772/75
Canvas   64 × 80 cm
Bequeathed by Louis La Caze, 1869

JEAN HONORÉ FRAGONARD
Grasse, 1732 – Paris, 1806
The bolt, circa 1778
Canvas   73 × 93 cm
Purchased in 1974

HUBERT ROBERT
Paris, 1733 – Paris, 1808
The Pont du Gard, exhibited at the Salon
   of 1787
Canvas   242 × 242 cm
Collection of Louis XVI

HUBERT ROBERT
Paris, 1733 – Paris, 1808
*Imaginary view of the Grande Galerie in the
   Louvre in ruins*, exhibited at the Salon
   of 1796
Canvas   114.5 × 146 cm
Purchased in 1975

The neo-classical period

Art historical research is again responsible for our ignoring traditional divisions by century, for the art of this period, which comprises the end of Louis XVI's reign, the Revolution and the Empire, has recently been re-assessed. Painting labelled 'neo-classical' was often thought to be cold and devoid of any true creativity, but recent exhibitions and publications have shown that it was, in fact, an extremely lively period, full of contradictions and rich in artistic personalities. French artists, above all Jacques Louis David, were the leaders of this European movement and no other museum can show the origins and development of neo-classical painting in France so comprehensively.

During Louis XVI's reign the policy of encouraging the painting of historical subjects, maintained by the Comte d'Angiviller, Surintendant des Bâtiments, meant that the King commissioned or purchased large paintings, often of Greek or Roman subjects destined to be woven as tapestries, several of which are still in the Louvre. The Direction des Bâtiments du Roi purchased two canvases by David which exploded upon the art scene and revolutionised painting of the period. These were *The oath of the Horatii* (p. 88) and *Brutus*, which stunned public and artists alike with their new plasticity and emotive power. At this time also Regnault's masterpiece of tortured elegance, *The Descent from the Cross* (p. 87), which had been commissioned as an altar-piece for the chapel at the Château de Fontainebleau, was purchased.

During the Revolution the government purchased a number of works that had been commissioned during the Monarchy, while paintings such as David's *Combat between Minerva and Mars* (second Prix de Rome in 1771) and Regnault's *Education of Achilles* (1782), were acquired with the Académie collection. Peyron's *The Funeral of Miltiades* (p. 87) and Madame Vigée-Lebrun's *Self-portrait with daughter* were among those seized from the Comte d'Angiviller, Gauffier's *Jacob and Laban's daughters* was seized from the Bernard collection, and David's signed copy of *Belisarius* from the Duchesse de Noailles.

During the Empire huge paintings of contemporary history were commissioned to glorify the Napoleonic era: David's *The Consecration of the Emperor Napoleon and Coronation of the Empress Josephine* (p. 91), and Gros' *Bonaparte visiting the plague-stricken at Jaffa* (p. 100) and *Napoleon on the battlefield of Eylau* (p. 99). The last two demonstrate the first important signs of the Romantic sensibility that was to pervade nineteenth-century Europe.

Nearly all the important acquisitions of *'la grande peinture'* of the neo-classical period came after the Restoration, when in 1818 the Musée de Luxembourg was created exclusively for the work of living artists and a deliberate acquisitions policy was established. Girodet's *The Deluge, The entombment of Atala* (p. 95) and *The sleep of Endymion* (p. 96) were bought in 1818, the large works by Guérin were bought between 1817 and 1830, except for *Phaedra and Hippolytus* which was bought at the Salon of 1802, Gérard's *Cupid and Psyche* (p. 96) was bought in 1822 and in 1826 Prud'hon's *Justice and Divine Vengeance pursuing Crime* (p. 94), executed for the Palais de Justice, was assigned to the Louvre by the City of Paris. In 1819 *The Sabine women* (p. 89) and *Leonidas at Thermopylae* were bought indirectly from David, by then in exile in Brussels. In 1823 the Comte d'Artois presented the painting of *Paris and Helen* that he had commissioned and purchased from David before the upheaval of the Revolution, and an unfinished masterpiece, the portrait of *Madame Récamier* (p. 90) was bought at the sale of David's studio in 1826, the year after his death.

In the second half of the nineteenth century portraits were the main contribution to the Louvre's collection of neo-classical art, often given or bequeathed by the artists' descendants, or by the sitters or their families. Two of Madame Vigée-Lebrun's masterpieces, another *Self-portrait* and the portrait of *Hubert Robert*, full of fire and tension (p. 90), were donated in 1843 by Madame Tripier-Le Franc, niece of the artist. David's portraits of *Monsieur Pécoul* and *Madame Pécoul* were acquired the next year and, in 1852, the artist Eugène Isabey presented a fine Gérard, the portrait of his father *Jean-Baptiste Isabey* (p. 97) and David's *Self-portrait*. In 1855 Madame Mongez bequeathed a double portrait by David of herself and her husband; David's *Madame Trudaine* (p. 90) was given in 1890 by Horace Paul Delaroche; and Gros' *Christine Boyer* (p. 99), Lucien Bonaparte's first wife, was acquired in 1894.

The twentieth century has added little to this exceptional collection, but the clear and fresh images of *Monsieur Sériziat* and *Madame Sériziat* by David were purchased in 1902. Acquisitions of note during this period are Prud'hon's *Young Zephyr* in the Schlichting bequest of 1915, David's only landscape, the exquisite *View of the Luxembourg gardens*, a gift of Bernheim-Jeune in 1912, and above all the Comte d'Espine's splendid collection given by his daughter, the Princesse de Croy, in 1930. The main feature of this collection was the group of landscapes painted in the open air by Michallon (27 works) and, more importantly, by Valenciennes (127 works) (p. 93). In the last fifty years more fine portraits have been acquired: *Madame de Verninac*, *Monsieur Meyer* and *General Bonaparte* by David; *Madame Lecerf* by Gérard and *Madame Pasteur* by Gros. In order to represent the whole range of neo-classical art a number of purchases in different areas have been made recently: Guérin's *The shepherds at Amyntas' tomb*, Regnault's *Socrates and Alcibiades* and the subtle *Still life with flowers* by the Lyonnais artist, Berjon.

This aim of covering the whole period in depth should remain paramount. Apart from the acknowledged masters whose works abound in the Louvre, many appealing artists, some only recently rediscovered, are scarcely represented if at all. The Louvre collection is undoubtedly without rival, and what needs to be done now is to give it the finishing touches and to represent the neo-classical period as completely as possible, showing all its many nuances.

JEAN-BAPTISTE REGNAULT
Paris, 1754 – Paris, 1829
The Descent from the Cross, 1789
Canvas   425 × 233 cm
Commissioned for the chapel in the
Château de Fontainebleau

JEAN-FRANÇOIS-PIERRE PEYRON
Aix-en-Provence, 1744 – Paris, 1814
The funeral of Miltiades, 1782
Canvas   98 × 136 cm
Seized during the French Revolution
from the collection of the Comte
d'Angiviller

JACQUES LOUIS DAVID
Paris, 1748 – Brussels, 1825
The oath of the Horatii, 1784
Canvas   330 × 425 cm
Collection of Louis XVI

Executed in Rome, this canvas was enthusiastically
received when it was exhibited at the Paris Salon of 1785.
Like Caravaggio's depictions of scenes from the life of St.
Matthew before, and Picasso's *Demoiselles d'Avignon* after,
The oath of the Horatii was to prove one of the great
turning-points in the history of art. The sober realism,
rigorous simplification of form and heroic tone of the
subject-matter were all to be of significant influence on
painting in the future.

JACQUES LOUIS DAVID
Paris, 1748 – Brussels, 1825
The Sabine women, 1799
Canvas   385 × 522 cm
Purchased in 1819

JEAN-GERMAIN DROUAIS
Paris, 1763 – Rome, 1788
Marius at Minturnae, 1786
Canvas   271 × 365 cm
Purchased in 1816

ELISABETH LOUISE VIGÉE-LEBRUN
Paris, 1755 – Paris, 1842
Hubert Robert, artist, 1788
Wood   105 × 84 cm
Presented by Madame Tripier le Franc, 1843

JACQUES LOUIS DAVID
Paris, 1748 – Brussels, 1825
Madame Trudaine, circa 1792(?)
Canvas   130 × 98 cm
Bequeathed by Horace Paul Delaroche, 1890

JACQUES LOUIS DAVID
Paris, 1748 – Brussels, 1825
Madame Récamier, 1800
Canvas   174 × 244 cm
Purchased in 1826

Jacques Louis David
Paris, 1748 – Brussels, 1825
*The Consecration of the Emperor Napoleon and Coronation of the
    Empress Josephine, 2nd December 1804, 1806/7*
Canvas   621 × 979 cm
Commissioned by Napoleon I

By judicious grouping of the figures and clear lighting,
David has avoided the muddle and confusion that could
have resulted from the depiction of such a huge crowd.
The consecration took place in the Cathedral of Notre
Dame, Paris, in the presence of Pope Pius VII. Although
the painting contains many individual realistic portraits, it
also achieves a general feeling of dignity and grandeur.
David could well have based the composition on that of
Rubens' *The coronation of Marie de Médicis*, originally in the
Palais du Luxembourg and now in the Louvre.

MARIE-GUILLEMINE BENOIST
Paris, 1768 – Paris, 1826
Portrait of a negress, exhibited at the Salon of 1800
Canvas   81 × 65 cm
Purchased in 1818

ANTOINE BERJON
Lyons, 1754 – Lyons, 1843
Still life with a basket of flowers, 1814
Canvas   66 × 50 cm
Purchased in 1974

LOUIS LÉOPOLD BOILLY
La Bassée, 1761 – Paris, 1845
Meeting of artists in Isabey's studio,
    exhibited at the Salon of 1798
Canvas   71.5 × 111 cm
Bequeathed by Monsieur Biesta-Monrival, 1901

PIERRE HENRI DE VALENCIENNES
Toulouse, 1750 – Paris, 1819
Storm at the edge of a lake, circa 1782/84
Paper on cardboard   39.8 × 52 cm
Collection of Comte de l'Espine;
presented by Princesse Louis de Croy,
1930

JOSEPH BIDAULD
Carpentras, 1758 – Montmorency, 1846
Landscape in Italy, 1793
Canvas   113 × 144 cm
Purchased at the Salon of 1793

PIERRE-PAUL PRUD'HON
Cluny, 1758 – Paris, 1823
The Empress Josephine, 1805
Canvas   244 × 179 cm
Collection of Napoleon III; presented in 1879

PIERRE-PAUL PRUD'HON
Cluny, 1758 – Paris, 1823
Justice and Divine Vengeance pursuing Crime, 1808
Canvas   244 × 294 cm
Commissioned for the Palais de Justice, Paris, and
    exchanged with the City of Paris in 1826

ANNE-LOUIS GIRODET DE ROUCY-TRIOSON
Montargis, 1767 – Paris, 1824
The entombment of Atala, 1808
Canvas   207 × 267 cm
Purchased in 1818

Atala, or the love of two savages in the desert, was published by
Chateaubriand in 1801 and inspired several painters. They
were seduced by the exotic subject-matter—the story of
the hopeless love of an Indian maiden, Atala, for a fellow
Indian, Chactas, set in Louisiana in the eighteenth century.
The tender and melancholy feeling in the painting and the
importance given to the contrast of light and shade,
diametrically opposed to David's style, is indicative of a
'pre-Romantic' sensibility, often one of the most attractive
aspects of painting during the neo-classical period. In an
even more dramatic and heightened manner, Prud'hon's
moonlit *Justice and Divine Vengeance pursuing Crime* shows
the same preoccupations, also very much 'anti-David'.

FRANÇOIS GÉRARD
Rome, 1770 – Paris, 1837
Cupid and Psyche, 1798
Canvas   186 × 132 cm
Purchased in 1822

ANNE-LOUIS GIRODET DE ROUCY-TRIOSON
Montargis, 1767 – Paris, 1824
The sleep of Endymion, 1793
Canvas   198 × 261 cm
Purchased in 1818

FRANÇOIS GÉRARD
Rome, 1770 – Paris, 1837
Jean-Baptiste Isabey, miniaturist, with his daughter, 1795
Canvas   194.5 × 130 cm
Presented by Eugène Isabey, 1852

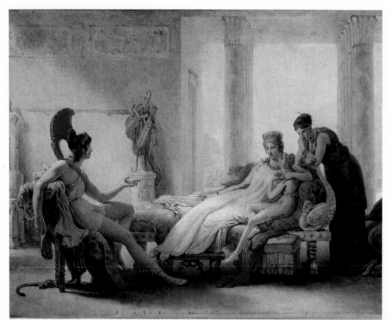

PIERRE-NARCISSE GUÉRIN
Paris, 1774 – Rome, 1833
Dido and Aeneas, sketch, 1815 or just before
Canvas   35 × 45 cm
Bequeathed by Adrien-Aimé Destouches, 1891

PIERRE-NARCISSE GUÉRIN
Paris, 1774 – Rome, 1833
The return of Marcus Sextus, 1799
Canvas   217 × 243 cm
Purchased in 1830

ANTOINE-JEAN GROS
Paris, 1771 – Meudon, 1835
Christine Boyer, circa 1800
Canvas 214 × 134 cm
Purchased in 1894

ANTOINE-JEAN GROS
Paris, 1771 – Meudon, 1835
Napoleon Bonaparte on the battlefield of Eylau, 1807, 1808
Canvas 521 × 784 cm
Commissioned after an open competition in 1807

ANTOINE-JEAN GROS
Paris, 1771 – Meudon, 1835
Napoleon Bonaparte visiting the plague-stricken at Jaffa, 1799,
   1804
Canvas   523 × 715 cm
Commissioned by the State

This vast scene, full of warmth and lyricism, is a good
example of the interest in the Orient instigated by
Napoleon's battle campaigns. The subject-matter is
actually little more than political propaganda, but its
execution and the strong emotional appeal achieved by the
simple treatment of the victims' fevered rapture, renders
this canvas the first great success of Romanticism in
painting.

The nineteenth century

uring the reigns of Louis XVIII and Charles X the collection acquired several masterpieces. by living artists purchased directly from the Salon. These included Ingres' *Roger and Angelica* in 1819, Delacroix's *Dante and Virgil* and *The massacre at Chios,* in 1822 and 1824 respectively, and the huge canvases by Delaroche, Devéria and Scheffer in 1828. The royal administration had a reputation for banal and conventional taste, but these acquisitions show that it was not necessarily always bad. In fact it could even be courageous, as in the famous purchase of the scandalous *The raft of the Medusa* by Géricault (p. 109), the subject of which was a contemporary event exploited by the Opposition to fight the existing régime. The canvas, purchased by Dedreux-Dorcy at the artist's posthumous sale in 1824, was sold the following year to the Museum for its original price. All contemporary paintings were exhibited in the Musée du Luxembourg, which opened as the 'Galerie royale du Luxembourg' in 1818 exclusively for the works of living artists. They were not hung in the Louvre until later.

A major contribution to the Louvre during the Restoration in terms of contemporary art was not in the field of easel painting but in that of decoration. Ambitious designs for the Museum's new galleries have left the building with an impressive series of huge painted ceilings which are perhaps still not sufficiently studied. Of particular beauty are the two parallel series of rooms along the first floor of the south wing of the Cour Carrée, which today is still known as the Musée Charles X and houses the collections of Greek, Roman and Egyptian art. The ceilings of the Conseil d'État in the west wing of the Cour Carrée (now the Department of Objets d'Art) were also painted at this time, as were those rooms near the principal staircases of the Louvre (Salle Percier et Fontaine, and Salle Duchâtel). Thus many history painters, sometimes more conscientious than inspired, but in whom interest is now once again being revived, are represented permanently in the Louvre by their most ambitious works without them having to purchase them or extract them from the reserve collections. Involved in this massive decorative scheme were not only ordinary artists such as Blondel, Picot, Alaux, M.M. Drolling and Mauzaisse, but also good painters such as Meynier, Heim, Schnetz, Abel de Pujol and Couder and true innovators such as E. Devéria, A.E. Fragonard (son of Jean-Honoré), L. Cogniet and H. Vernet (grandson of Claude-Joseph). Neither should the last and possibly less accomplished works by the brilliant Baron Gros be forgotten, nor one of Ingres' most elaborate compositions (p. 107), *The apotheosis of Homer.* This last-mentioned work was removed during the artist's lifetime and transformed into an easel painting for the Exposition Universelle of 1855 and was replaced by a copy painted by the Balze brothers.

During Louis-Philippe's reign the most important scheme was the Musée historique in the Château de Versailles, and the major commissions during this period were always destined for Versailles. The project was executed on a hitherto unprecedented scale which involved not only the decoration of a museum as had just been done at the Louvre under

Charles x, but the formation of an entire collection of exhibits at the same time, all with a pomp not seen since the time of Louis xiv. The Galérie des Batailles alone is a matter for wonder. In 1885 the Louvre acquired Delacroix's *The entry of the Crusaders into Constantinople*, from the museum in Versailles and this unforgettable canvas, full of melancholy and passion, is a fitting echo of Veronese's and Rubens' great works hanging nearby.

The most beautiful Delacroixs continued to be purchased at the Salon: *The women of Algiers* (p. 112) in 1834, and *The Jewish wedding* in 1841. His masterpiece, *Liberty guiding the people* (p. 111), one of the most glorious paintings in the Louvre, had been purchased by Louis-Philippe in 1831. However, the influence of the painting's message was so feared by the Government that it was only exhibited for a few weeks in the Musée du Luxembourg. It was then returned to Delacroix and remained hidden except for a brief time in 1849. It was later shown at the Exposition Universelle of 1855, was exhibited at the Musée du Luxembourg again from 1861 and finally reached the Louvre in 1874. Paradoxically, Delacroix's great rival, Ingres, despite being a classical painter and ardent follower of Raphael, was much less well treated by the State, who bought few of his works; the scandalous and revolutionary Delacroix, prime exponent of Romantic art, fared much better. Ingres' portrait of *Cherubini* was purchased in 1842, and he was commissioned to paint *The Virgin with Eucharistic wafer*, which he did not complete until 1854. Louis-Philippe's major contribution to the Louvre's collection of works by Ingres was the fascinating series of twenty-five cartoons for the stained glass windows in the chapels of Saint-Ferdinand de Paris and Saint-Louis de Dreux executed between 1842 and 1844. Couture's *The Romans of the decadence* (p. 124), commissioned by the State, was purchased in 1847.

The brief but generous Republic of 1848 purchased works by Géricault, five in 1849, and the vast, sublime images of *The officer of the Imperial Guard charging* and *The wounded officer of the Imperial Guard leaving the battlefield* (p. 108) at the sale of Louis-Philippe's possessions in 1851, as well as commissioning Duban to execute the restoration of the Galerie d'Apollon. The painted decoration was not completed and the central panel of the vaulted ceiling was painted by Delacroix between 1850 and 1851 with a scene depicting *Apollo vanquishing the Python* (p. 113). Full of innovative lyricism, it is also magnificently in keeping with the paintings by Le Brun and eighteenth-century masters which surround it.

The acquisitions policy of the Second Empire was eclectic. Works by academic and 'Salon' artists such as Delaunay, Baudry, Carolus-Duran, Gérôme, Lenepveu and Meissonier were acquired, but also, more adventurously, two Corots, *The dance of the nymphs* in 1851 and the famous *Souvenir de Mortefontaine* (p. 116) at the Salon of 1864. Gustave Moreau's *Orpheus* (p. 125), which entered the Musée du Luxembourg in 1867, was yet more avant-garde. However, works of the great contemporary innovators of the Realist movement, who rejected official academic teaching, were not allowed into the Museum. Neither Millet, Courbet, Daumier, Troyon nor Dupré were exhibited.

Not until the end of the century, and after the artists' deaths, was this injustice rectified. Courbet's *The wave* was purchased in 1878, and many masterpieces, amongst them *The wounded man* (p. 120), were bought at the sale of his studio in 1881. In that same year Juliette Courbet presented *The burial at Ornans* (p. 120), one of her brother's most important canvases. Several works by Millet were acquired at his posthumous sale in 1875; Madame Hartmann gave *Spring* (p. 119) in 1887 and Madame Pommery *The gleaners* in 1890. It was also after Ingres' death that several of his masterpieces came into the collection: among bequests were the three portraits of the Rivière family (p. 105) by Monsieur and Madame Rivière's daughter-in-law in 1870; *Oedipus* and *The spring* bequeathed by the Comtesse Ducharel in 1878; and *Cordier* by Comtesse Mortier in 1886. Purchases included the portrait of *Monsieur Bochet* in 1878, the *Valpinçon bather* in 1879, the famous *Monsieur Bertin* (p. 107) and *The 'grande odalisque'* (p. 106) in 1899. The series was crowned by the Société des Amis du Louvre's gift of *The Turkish bath* (p. 106) in 1911.

Three large gifts in the early years of this century meant that big collections of small or medium-sized paintings entered the Louvre and ensured magnificent representation of artists such as Corot, Delacroix, Decamps, Millet and the Barbizon School of landscape painters. In 1902, Thomy Thiéry, an Englishman of French origin from Mauritius living in Paris, bequeathed a collection consisting entirely of nineteenth-century paintings, among them Delacroix's *Medea*, *The abduction of Rebecca*, nine small canvases and many splendid Corots and Barbizon paintings. Even richer and more varied was the collection given by Étienne Moreau-Nélaton in 1906. It comprised no less than thirty-seven superbly selected Corots and several masterpieces by Delacroix, including *Still life with a lobster* and *Young girl in the graveyard*, as well as a sketch by Géricault for *The raft of the Medusa* and Daumier's Michelangelesque *The Republic* (p. 118). The Moreau-Nélaton collection included the most avant-garde and truly innovative of contemporary art and it was through this collection that the Louvre acquired paintings by Monet and by Berthe Morisot, Sisley and Pissarro. The whole collection was exhibited in the Musée des Arts Décoratifs for a long time and did not enter the Louvre until 1934. The third gift was that of Alfred Chauchard in 1909, a fine collection of works by Corot, Delacroix, Millet, Diaz, Decamps, Dupré, Daubigny and Meissonier often acquired at high prices. The sum of 800,000 francs paid by Chauchard in 1889 for Millet's *Angelus* (p. 119) caused a sensation at the time. The Camondo bequest in 1911 also included fine Delacroixs and Corots, as well as splendid Impressionists.

After the First World War the Louvre made several spectacular acquisitions in the field of nineteenth-century art. Courbet's masterpiece, *The artist's studio* (p. 121), was purchased in 1920 with the help of both a public subscription and the Société des Amis du Louvre, and Delacroix's *The death of Sardanapalus* (p. 111), one of the greatest expressions of Romantic art, was purchased the following year. The generosity of owners, descendants of great artists, keen to see their forebears' oeuvre well represented in the Louvre, or of private collectors, has continued to this day. In the first category, Baron Arthur Chassériau should be mentioned above all. His fine gift in 1918 and bequest in 1933/34 amounted to forty-three canvases by his uncle showing the whole range of that artist's genius (p. 115). During the same period, between 1926 and 1932, the joint action of the Société des Amis du Louvre and the Société Chassériau ensured that the damaged paintings from the staircase in the Cour des Comptes, burnt in 1871, should be saved and preserved in the Louvre.

Recently private collectors have been particularly generous. In 1942 Carlos de Beistegui presented Ingres' portraits of *Bartolini* and *Madame Panckoucke*, and two small works by Meissonier, of which one was *The barricade* (p. 125); in 1965 Baronne Gourgaud gave works by Corot and two splendid works by Delacroix and Daumier; James N.B. Hill gave, in 1962 and bequeathed in 1978, paintings by Troyon, Corot and Millet; and portraits of *Pierre-Joseph Prudhon* and *Madame Prudhon* by Courbet were presented by their grand-daughters in 1958. Two other fine works by Courbet, *Still life with trout* and *Nude figure with a dog* have recently been received in lieu of death duties (1978 and 1979). In 1979 the Louvre's dazzling collection of works by Delacroix was augmented by the landscape it still needed, *The sea from the cliffs at Dieppe* (p. 112), an extraordinary painting like a Claude Monet view from the hand of Titian.

As the vast sphere of nineteenth-century art still has many scantly-explored areas, it is difficult to form a clear idea of exactly what the Louvre should exhibit in order to give an accurate impression of the century and to emphasise its particular innovations. The Louvre, of course, favours the acknowledged masters, and is apt to mirror the taste of late nineteenth-century collectors. However, there is now room for greater variety in the collection and a more comprehensive coverage of the period, for yet again taste has changed.

The balance of nineteenth-century painting in the Louvre is going to alter fundamentally with the opening of the museum of nineteenth-century art in the old Gare d'Orsay. The work of Courbet, Millet, Daumier and landscapists of the Barbizon School will go to the new museum, as will that of Puvis de Chavannes, Moreau, Couture, Meissonier and the so-called 'academic' painters. Certain canvases by Ingres, Delacroix, Chassériau and Corot will also go, but the major works of the first half of the century, especially the unique series of vast canvases, will continue to be exhibited in the Louvre to be viewed and compared with the masterpieces of the past centuries.

JEAN AUGUSTE DOMINIQUE INGRES
Montauban, 1780 – Paris, 1867
Mademoiselle Rivière, exhibited at the Salon of 1806
Canvas   100 × 70 cm
Bequeathed by Madame Rivière, 1870

JEAN AUGUSTE DOMINIQUE INGRES
Montauban, 1780 – Paris, 1867
The Turkish bath, 1862
Canvas on wood   diameter 108 cm
Presented by the Société des Amis du Louvre, 1911

JEAN AUGUSTE DOMINIQUE INGRES
Montauban, 1780 – Paris, 1867
The 'grande odalisque', 1814
Canvas   91 × 162 cm
Purchased in 1899

The female nude was a subject that interested Ingres all his life. *The Turkish bath*, the last of his many variations on the theme, shows, as does *The 'grande odalisque'*, the fascination exerted by the Orient throughout the nineteenth century. In *The apotheosis of Homer* Ingres has surrounded Homer, author of *The Odyssey*, with all the great writers and artists of Antiquity, and placed those of modern times further down. Only Raphael, whom Ingres saw as the embodiment of the perfect painter, is allowed to feature with the venerable artists of ancient times.

JEAN AUGUSTE DOMINIQUE INGRES
Montauban, 1780 – Paris, 1867
Monsieur Bertin, 1832
Canvas   116 × 95 cm
Purchased in 1897

JEAN AUGUSTE DOMINIQUE INGRES
Montauban, 1780 – Paris, 1867
The apotheosis of Homer, 1827
Canvas   386 × 512 cm
Originally a ceiling painting in the Salle Clarac in the Louvre,
    commissioned in 1826

THÉODORE GÉRICAULT
Rouen, 1781 – Paris, 1824
The wounded officer of the Imperial Guard leaving the battlefield,
    exhibited at the Salon of 1814
Canvas   358 × 294 cm
Purchased in 1851

THÉODORE GÉRICAULT
Rouen, 1781 – Paris, 1824
The raft of the Medusa, exhibited at the Salon of 1819
Canvas 491 × 716 cm
Purchased in 1824

This painting was a *'succès de scandale'* at the Salon of 1819, recalling the wreck of the *Medusa* in 1816 and the shameful inability of the captain to save his passengers, except a few who were crowded together on a raft. After a long time at sea, further deaths and even instances of cannibalism, the survivors were finally rescued. Géricault made several studies of dying people and corpses in hospitals before executing this sublime painting—one of the greatest visual interpretations of human suffering.

THÉODORE GÉRICAULT
Rouen, 1781 – Paris, 1824
The madwoman, circa 1822
Canvas   77 × 64.5 cm
Presented by the Société des Amis du
    Louvre, 1938

THÉODORE GÉRICAULT
Rouen, 1781 – Paris, 1824
The plaster kiln, circa 1822/23
Canvas   50 × 61 cm
Purchased in 1849

EUGÈNE DELACROIX
Charenton–Saint-Maurice, 1798 –
    Paris, 1863
The death of Sardanapalus, exhibited at
    the Salon of 1827/28
Canvas   392 × 496 cm
Purchased in 1921

EUGÈNE DELACROIX
Charenton–Saint-Maurice, 1798 – Paris,
1863
Liberty guiding the people, 28th July 1830,
1830
Canvas   260 × 325 cm
Purchased at the Salon of 1831

EUGÈNE DELACROIX
Charenton-Saint-Maurice, 1798 –
   Paris, 1863
The sea from the cliffs at Dieppe, 1852(?)
Cardboard on wood   35 × 51 cm
Bequeathed by Marcel Beurdeley, 1979

EUGÈNE DELACROIX
Charenton-Saint-Maurice, 1798 – Paris, 1863
The women of Algiers, 1834
Canvas   180 × 229 cm
Purchased at the Salon of 1834

Eugène Delacroix
Charenton-Saint-Maurice, 1798 – Paris, 1863
Apollo vanquishing the Python, 1850/51
Mural painting   About 800 × 750 cm
Central panel of the vaulted ceiling of the Galerie d'Apollon
    in the Louvre

One of Delacroix's lesser-known masterpieces, the
subject-matter was dictated by its destination. *Apollo
vanquishing the Python* shows the painter working in a direct
line from the great decorators of the seventeenth and
eighteenth centuries, without losing any of his own ardour
or lyricism.

113

ARY SCHEFFER
Dordrecht, 1795 – Argenteuil, 1858
The ghosts of Paolo and Francesca appear to Dante and Virgil, 1855 (copy
    by the artist of a painting first executed in 1822)
Canvas   171 × 239 cm
Bequeathed by Madame Marjolin-Scheffer, 1900

HIPPOLYTE FLANDRIN
Lyons, 1809 – Paris, 1864
Young man by the sea, 1837
Canvas   98 × 124 cm
Entered the Musée de Luxembourg in
    1857

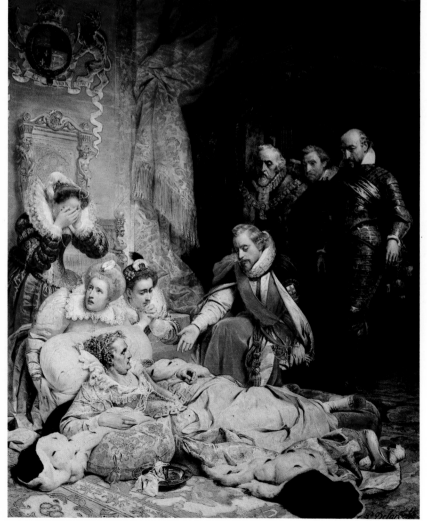

PAUL DELAROCHE
Paris, 1797 – Paris, 1856
*The death of Elizabeth I, Queen of
    England*, 1828
Canvas   422 × 343 cm
Purchased at the Salon of 1827/28

THÉODORE CHASSÉRIAU
Sainte-Barbe-de-Samana, 1819 – Paris, 1856
The two sisters (the artist's sisters), 1843
Canvas   180 × 135 cm
Bequeathed by Baron and Baronne Arthur Chassériau, 1918

THÉODORE CHASSÉRIAU
Sainte-Barbe-de-Samana, 1819 – Paris, 1856
The toilet of Esther, 1841
Canvas   45.5 × 35.5 cm
Bequeathed by Baron Arthur Chassériau, 1934

THÉODORE CHASSÉRIAU
Sainte-Barbe-de-Samana, 1819 –
Paris, 1856
Peace, between 1844 and 1848
Canvas   340 × 362 cm
Fragment from the decoration of
the building of the Cour des
Comptes, burnt in 1871
Bequeathed by the Chassériau
Committee, 1903

JEAN-BAPTISTE CAMILLE COROT
Paris, 1796 – Paris, 1875
Volterra, 1834
Canvas   70.5 × 94 cm
Bequeathed by Étienne Moreau-
   Nélaton, 1906

JEAN-BAPTISTE CAMILLE COROT
Paris, 1796 – Paris, 1875
Souvenir de Mortefontaine, exhibited at the Salon of 1864
Canvas   65 × 89 cm
Purchased at the Salon of 1864

JEAN-BAPTISTE CAMILLE COROT
Paris, 1796 – Paris, 1875
Chartres Cathedral, 1830, retouched in 1872
Canvas   64 × 51.5 cm
Bequeathed by Étienne Moreau-Nélaton, 1906

Jean-Baptiste Camille Corot
Paris, 1796 – Paris, 1875
Woman in blue, 1874
Canvas   80 × 50.5 cm
Purchased in 1912

The female figures executed by Corot entirely for his own
enjoyment, particularly at the end of his life, are now often
admired as much, if not more, than the landscapes for
which he is traditionally famous. One of the last and
perhaps the most beautiful of these female studies,
unknown to the public during Corot's lifetime, is the
Woman in blue, a triumph in the handling of paint and a fine
example of strength of composition and grandiose
simplicity.

HONORÉ DAUMIER
Marseilles, 1808 – Valmondois, 1879
The Republic, 1848
Canvas   73 × 60 cm
Bequeathed by Étienne Moreau-Nélaton, 1906

HONORÉ DAUMIER
Marseilles 1808 – Valmondois, 1879
*'The thieves and the ass', episode from the fable by La Fontaine,
circa 1848/50(?)*
Canvas   58.5 × 56 cm   Purchased in 1893

JEAN-FRANÇOIS MILLET
Gruchy, 1814 – Barbizon, 1875
The gleaners, exhibited at the Salon of 1857
Canvas   83.7 × 111 cm
Bequeathed by Madame Pommery, 1890

JEAN-FRANÇOIS MILLET
Gruchy, 1814 – Barbizon, 1875
The Angelus, 1857/59
Canvas   55.5 × 66 cm
Bequeathed by Alfred Chauchard, 1909

JEAN-FRANÇOIS MILLET
Gruchy, 1814 – Barbizon, 1875
Spring, 1868/73
Canvas   86 × 111 cm
Bequeathed by Madame Frédéric Hartmann, 1887

◄

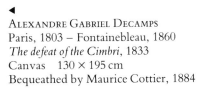

ALEXANDRE GABRIEL DECAMPS
Paris, 1803 – Fontainebleau, 1860
The defeat of the Cimbri, 1833
Canvas   130 × 195 cm
Bequeathed by Maurice Cottier, 1884

GUSTAVE COURBET
Ornans, 1817 – La Tour-de-Pfeilz, 1877
The wounded man, 1844(?)
Canvas   81.5 × 97.5 cm
Purchased in 1881

GUSTAVE COURBET
Ornans, 1817 – La Tour-de-Pfeilz, 1877
The burial at Ornans, 1849/50
Canvas   315 × 668 cm
Presented by Juliette Courbet, 1881

GUSTAVE COURBET
Ornans, 1817 – La Tour-de-Pfeilz, 1877
The artist's studio, 1855
Canvas   361 × 598 cm
Purchased in 1920

GUSTAVE COURBET
Ornans, 1817 – La Tour-de-Pfeilz, 1877
The cliffs at Etretat after a storm, 1870
Canvas   133 × 162 cm
Presented by the Office des Biens Privés, 1950

As well as huge subjects like *The burial at Ornans* or *The artist's studio* (pp. 120 and 121), which are often difficult to understand, Courbet was able to paint pure landscape. *The cliffs at Etretat* shows his freshness and accuracy of lighting effects, and also his ability to paint alternately with an almost sculptural touch or one of delicate nuances.

THÉODORE ROUSSEAU
Paris, 1812 – Barbizon, 1867
Group of oak trees, Apremont, 1852
Canvas   63.5 × 99.5 cm
Bequeathed by Thomy Thiéry, 1902

CHARLES-FRANÇOIS DAUBIGNY
Paris, 1817 – Paris, 1878
The floodgate at Optevoz, 1859
Canvas   48.5 × 73 cm
Bequeathed by Thomy Thiéry, 1902

THOMAS COUTURE
Senlis, 1815 – Villiers-le-Bel, 1879
The Romans of the decadence, 1847
Canvas   466 × 775 cm
Purchased at the Salon of 1847

JEAN–LÉON GÉRÔME
Vesoul, 1824 – Paris, 1904
The cock fight, 1846
Canvas   143 × 204 cm
Transferred from the Musée du
    Luxembourg, 1920

GUSTAVE MOREAU
Paris, 1826 – Paris, 1893
Orpheus, 1865
Wood   154 × 99.5 cm
Presented to the Musée du Luxembourg by the
Ministry of Arts, 1867

ERNEST MEISSONIER
Lyons, 1815 – Paris, 1891
The barricade, June 1848, exhibited at the Salon of 1850/51
Canvas   29 × 22 cm
Bequeathed by Carlos de Beistegui, 1942

PIERRE PUVIS DE CHAVANNES
Lyons, 1824 – Paris, 1898
The poor fisherman, 1881
Canvas   155.5 × 192.5 cm
Purchased in 1887

Generally badly received in the nineteenth century, often misunderstood even today because of its 'sentimental' subject-matter, *The poor fisherman* actually shows how great an innovator Puvis de Chavannes was. The subtle arrangement of the simplified and rather stilted forms and the limited range of low-keyed, soft colours are similar to those of the Nabis at the very end of the century, or the young Picasso a few years later.

View of the Grande Galerie from an etching published in 1822

European paintings in the Louvre

HUBERT ROBERT
Paris, 1733—Paris, 1808
View of the Grande Galerie of the Louvre, 1796
Canvas 115 × 145 cm
Purchased in 1975

Hubert Robert painted many views, both real and imaginary, of the Grande Galerie of the Louvre. His imaginary views really constitute a set of designs for an ideal museum. When he painted this picture (the finest in the series) in 1796, the Gallery was nothing but an interminably long corridor, lit only by side windows, which linked the Louvre to the Tuileries. The architects who were later responsible for the lighting and redecoration of the Grande Galerie were merely executing the original ideas of Hubert Robert. In this painting several of the masterpieces of the Muséum Central can be recognised, notably Raphael's *The Holy Family of François I* and Titian's *Entombment*.

Introduction

Cézanne once said 'It seems to me that the Louvre has all we need, that everything can be loved and understood there'. Few of the great museums of the world contain such varied collections of all schools of European painting from the end of the thirteenth to the nineteenth century, and illustrate such diverse styles and formats. The collections range from small, intimate paintings to monumental canvases, from frescoes to whole decorative schemes, and offer examples of schools rarely represented outside their native countries. The wide range of the collection, despite the inevitable serious gaps and weaker sections, is the result of the long history of the formation of the collection over more than four and a half centuries and of the fact that it was a royal collection before it became a national museum. The nineteenth- and twentieth-century acquisitions followed the evolution of taste and the discovery of the discipline of art history, and the royal collection was thus complemented and balanced by previously unknown or disregarded paintings.

It is often forgotten that the collection originated in the sixteenth century with a 'museum of modern art'. François I followed the example of his predecessor Louis XII, and with a bravado which was the envy of other European monarchs approached the most prestigious living artists, either buying their paintings or bringing them from Italy to work for him. The patronage of contemporary artists continued to sustain the royal collection, and the then 'Old Masters' were also purchased.

Not only does François I's collection of contemporary Italian paintings, given place of honour at the Château de Fontainebleau, testify to the personal taste of an enlightened prince, but it is also one of the clearest indications of the introduction from Italy into France of the Renaissance. François I called upon several French and Flemish painters (Jean Clouet and Joos van Cleve, for example), as Henri II and Cathérine de Médicis were to do with François Clouet, but it would seem that this was solely for portraiture, a field in which the competence of Northern artists was acknowledged. It did not, nevertheless, prevent the King from asking Titian to paint his portrait.

After the reign of Henri IV, who used French artists or artists working in France, such as Ambroise Dubois, for the decoration of his residences, a short but brilliant period of royal patronage was initiated by Marie de Médicis. She commissioned Rubens to decorate the gallery of the Palais du Luxembourg in 1625 and she also employed another Flemish artist, Pourbus, and the Italian, Gentileschi, at a time when the most promising young French painters such as Vouet, Poussin, and Claude Lorrain were themselves in Italy and as yet unrecognised.

The great tradition of François I was resumed by Louis XIV. As soon as he took power in 1661, the King began to enrich the royal collection, advised by his minister Colbert, until its magnificence soon reflected that of the reign of the Sun King himself. This was largely thanks to two spectacular acquisitions: a large part of Cardinal Mazarin's famous collection, and in 1662 and 1671 that of the banker Everhard Jabach. Masterpieces of the Italian Renaissance which had always been revered (works by Leonardo, Raphael, and Titian and also by Correggio and Veronese), most of which had come from the collection of Charles I of England, were reunited with those from François I's collection, while the work of more recent artists such as Caravaggio and Guido Reni also entered the royal collection. It was continually enriched with other sixteenth-century paintings, particularly by the great Venetian artists, and by paintings from seventeenth-century Rome and Bologna which appealed to the French taste for classicism; a taste nurtured by the art of Poussin, Claude, Le Brun, and their followers. The northern Renaissance is also well represented in the collection of Louis XIV with an impressive series of portraits by Holbein and works by Beham and Anthonio Moro. The acquisition of Dutch and Flemish art of the seventeenth century indicates the change in taste of both collectors and young artists themselves at the end of the century. More colourful and sensual painting, which exhibits not so much idealisation but rather expressive animation and, indeed, the picturesque, is exemplified by the paintings of Rembrandt, Rubens, and van Dyck.

Although magnificent private collections, which were to be gold mines for the princely galleries of Germany, for Catherine the Great, and for British collectors, were assembled under Louis XV, and although Paris became one of the centres of European art, the Cabinet du Roi (King's collection) hardly increased at all. Some foreign paintings, mostly bought from the estate of the Prince de Carignan in 1742, were added, and constituted an excellent selection, dominated by Flemish and Dutch art.

Towards the middle of the eighteenth century the public began to demand that the royal collections should be on general view. The idea of installing a suitable museum in the old palace of the Louvre materialised under Louis XVI. The Surintendant des Bâtiments, the Comte d'Angiviller, began a programme of acquisitions. His policy was not just a case of enriching the King's gallery with costly works in order to boost royal prestige; it was a deliberate effort to build up a more representative collection of the different schools of painting as they were known and appreciated at the time. The Age of Reason and of Diderot's 'Encyclopaedia' demanded this approach. Additions to the foreign collection were principally to the Flemish and especially to the Dutch seventeenth-century sections. The Italian 'primitives' were still not appreciated, but there was another innovation in the acquisition of Spanish painting, at last represented in the royal collection by Murillo.

The project was completed by the French Revolution. The 'Muséum Central des Arts' was opened in the Louvre in 1793. The resources of the royal collection, now the national collection, were soon augmented by numerous paintings seized from churches or collectors who had emigrated and then, in the wake of French military victories, by masterpieces seized in Flanders and Holland, Italy and Germany. It was thus that a fabulous museum, called the Musée Napoléon from 1803, was founded. It was dominated by foreign art: masters of the Renaissance and seventeenth century in Italy, Flanders, and Holland, but also early Flemish and early Italian masters and painters of the German Renaissance, rescued at last from oblivion. Today's international moral code would condemn such an enterprise, yet it would be wrong to attribute it simply to the ritual plundering of victorious armies. The Musée Napoléon was undoubtedly formed in the spirit of its creators, above all of its admirable director,

Vivant Denon, as a High Temple of Art for the edification of the citizens of Imperial Europe. It was designed to illustrate the moral and intellectual progress which stemmed from the Revolution: in the words of Denon, the 'comparison of the efforts of the human spirit throughout the centuries'. The creation of other museums in the main provincial towns (such as Brussels, Geneva, Mainz, and Milan) with Parisian funds conformed to the same nobly educative policy.

In 1815, after Waterloo, representatives sent by the beleaguered countries took back more than five thousand works of art. Only about a hundred paintings escaped restitution and were left in the Louvre by the allies of France. However, the wealth of its reserves ensured the survival of the Museum. During the Restoration and the July Monarchy efforts were either directed elsewhere, to the creation under Louis XVIII of the Musée du Luxembourg for living artists, and, under Louis-Philippe, of the Musée de l'histoire de France at Versailles, or were without lasting benefit for the national heritage, as in the establishment of Louis-Philippe's Spanish collection, returned to the Orleans family after 1848 and shortly afterwards sold in England. But after the Revolution of 1848 and under the Second Empire, the Museum took on a new lease of life. Thereafter, and until the First World War, the curators were to be in competition with their English and German colleagues, and later American collectors, for the purchase of paintings missing in the collection. The history of art, now an acknowledged academic discipline, had begun to define the true perspectives of European painting, from early masters to the eighteenth century, resurrecting this or that artist or entire school from years of neglect. The continual purchases of collectors increased the rarity of works on the market, but the Louvre gradually filled some of the gaps in its collection, especially in the field of 'primitives'. The purchase of the Campana collection in 1863 consisted of about a hundred such 'primitive' Italian panels of the fourteenth and fifteenth centuries. The Spanish and English collections were also increased and Italian eighteenth-century paintings were bought. Simultaneously, the great variety in taste of the connoisseurs who generously gave or bequeathed works to the Louvre balanced and diversified the representation of different schools, whether recently brought to light or traditionally appreciated. In the first rank of these connoisseurs must be placed Dr La Caze, whose collection entered the Louvre in 1869.

Throughout the nineteenth century the abundance of French painting and its influence internationally on both official and avant-garde art distracted museum curators and French collectors alike from the contemporary art of other countries. It was only from the end of the century that works representative of most of the European countries and of the United States were acquired for the Musée du Luxembourg (later these paintings were to form a special museum for modern foreign schools at the Musée du Jeu de Paume). This contemporary harvest was rich but uneven. Whistler's *The artist's mother*, and remarkable paintings by Winslow Homer, Watts, and Pelizza da Volpedo were acquired to the exclusion of Klimt or Munch, the most original of the Symbolists. These paintings are now destined for the future Musée d'Orsay, where they will join the nation's French works of the same period now on view at the Jeu de Paume, the Louvre, and the Palais de Tokyo.

After 1918 the era of great purchases seemed to be over. The Louvre bought Dürer's *Self portrait*, but lack of funds, despite the constant help and foresight of the Société des Amis du Louvre, prevented the possibility of acquiring masterpieces from private collections which foreign museums and art lovers, especially Americans, were able to acquire. Yet on the eve of the Second World War the spirit of the Museum was revived once again. A general reorganisation, which continued after the War, was begun. Several important donations from great and established collections (Rothschild, Groult, Péreire) or more recent ones (Beistegui, Nicolas, Lyon, Salavin) enriched different sections of the foreign schools. Less stringent credit terms and new legal provisions, which authorised the gift of works of art in lieu of death duties and thus secured for the Louvre major works by Filippino Lippi, Rubens, and Goya, enabled the pursuit of a new programme of acquisitions. Today the curators of the Louvre, like their predecessors, strive to present a complete picture of European painting by adding to and constantly reassessing the collection.

The fourteenth and fifteenth centuries in Italy

From the time of the High Renaissance, the early Italian masters or 'primitives' had been neglected in favour of classicism. Artists earlier than Perugino or Leonardo were absent from the French royal collections and from those of other European princes. The resurrection of the Trecento and Quattrocento artists began with the establishment of the Musée Napoléon at the beginning of the nineteenth century. Certain French art historians like Seroux d'Agincourt, or connoisseurs such as Artaud de Montor and Cacault, were amongst the pioneers of a rediscovery which was to earn the admiration of the Nazarenes in Germany and the exponents of the 'style troubadour' in France. This admiration did not become general before about 1825, although works by Mantegna and Giovanni Bellini had been included in the first convoys of paintings brought back from Italy in 1798 by the triumphant Napoleonic armies. The importance of the primitive Italian school of the remote Middle Ages was sensed by Vivant Denon, who was always anxious to broaden the horizons of his Museum. He went to Italy in 1811 to choose a series of fifteenth-century Florentine altarpieces by Fra Angelico (p 142), Filippo Lippi (p 143), Ghirlandaio, Lorenzo di Credi, and even older works, notably the altarpieces by Cimabue (p 137) and Giotto (p 138) from the church of San Francesco in Pisa. In Genoa he bought the triptych now attributed to Carlo Braccesco (p 152). When in 1815 the allies organised a large scale operation to return works of art to their countries of origin, this section of the Museum was less disrupted than most. The Louvre kept the *Madonna of Victory* and one of the panels (p 146) of the predella of the San Zeno altarpiece by Mantegna, as well as the Florentine altarpieces assembled by Vivant Denon which the authorities of the city gave to the Museum.

The following period of the Restoration and the July Monarchy was notoriously unprofitable for old collections. However, several isolated purchases deserve mention: the panels by the Master of the Codex of St George (p 139) and the Master of Ovile from the collection of the troubadour painter Pierre-Henri Révoil; the *Birth of St John* by Signorelli in 1824; and, above all, the *Carrying of the Cross* by Simone Martini (p 139) in 1834. This, like the other small panels from the same polyptych (now in the Fine Arts Museum, Antwerp), was acquired in Dijon and came from the Carthusian monastery of Champmol. The price of this exquisite masterpiece indicates the low regard in which the primitives were held at this time by all but a few isolated connoisseurs. The work was bought for the modest sum of 200 francs, while there was no hesitation in paying 250,000 francs for the *Nativity* by Spagna, a second-rate Umbrian painter whose work was overshadowed by that of Perugino and Raphael.

Under the Second Empire, the affair of the Campana collection caused a scandal which was to have important consequences for the Louvre. The Marquis Campana (1807–80), director of an important banking concern in Rome, had accumulated a fantastic collection of antiques and paintings by early masters in his palaces. Driven by his passion for collecting, he had begun to borrow increasingly large sums of money from the company which he directed, 'investing' them in his own collection. In 1857 the accounts were checked and the deficit revealed. Campana was arrested and sentenced to banishment and his collections were put up for sale. After secret negotiations and stiff competition between several great European museums, the collection of some 11,835 objects, including 646 paintings, was bought by Napoleon III for the vast sum of 4,360,400 francs. At first exhibited in its entirety at the Palais de l'Industrie (from 1862), this unique collection was then brutally divided (in 1863, 1872, and 1876) between various provincial museums, the Louvre retaining only about a hundred Trecento and Quattrocento paintings. This senseless dispersal, decried in vain at the time by many artists, including Ingres and Delacroix, has now been remedied by regrouping the 300 primitives which had been scattered among local museums at the Petit Palais in Avignon, opened in 1976. The Campana collection in the Louvre is very varied, with special emphasis on the Tuscan School and on the Venetian and other northern Schools. Other centres of art, less appreciated and judged provincial at the time of the dispersal of the collection, are better represented at Avignon, and range from the Giottesque Florentine painters such as Bernardo Daddi to Bartolommeo Vivarini and Mantegna. Among the masterpieces from the collection in the Louvre are Uccello's *Battle* (p 145), Cosimo Tura's *Pietà* (p 148), and the series of *Famous men* from the Palazzo Ducale at Urbino by Justus of Ghent and Pedro Berruguete.

When these paintings entered the Louvre, the battle for the Italian primitives had been won. The fourteenth and fifteenth centuries, better known thanks to the research of the art historians Crowe and Cavalcaselle and later of Berenson, were worshipped by the English Pre-Raphaelites and their followers, and became henceforth the object of a universal craze. The keepers of the Louvre devoted themselves to the completion of the collections. Without managing to create a panorama as complete as their colleagues at the National Gallery in London, they nevertheless acquired distinguished works by Antonello da Messina, Baldovinetti (p 145), Jacopo (p 141) and Giovanni Bellini, Pisanello (p 141), and Ghirlandaio (p 151), and also successfully acquired the allegorical frescoes by Fra Angelico from the convent of San Domenico in Fiesole. In 1910 the town of Aigueperse sold to the Louvre Mantegna's *St Sebastian*, which had belonged to the Gonzaga-Montpensier family. There were other donations, notably the bequest of the Baronne Nathaniel de Rothschild (Ercole de' Roberti) at the same time.

It was not until the mid-1950s, when the initial enthusiasm for purchases of Italian primitives by American collectors had passed, that there were noteworthy acquisitions in this field once again. Among these treasures were the three great panels of the altarpiece from Borgo San Sepolcro by Sassetta (1956), joined fortuitously in 1970 by one of the paintings of the predella of the same polyptych; the *Calvary* by Giovanni Bellini (p 148) and the *Story of Esther* by Filippino Lippi (p 151), acquired in 1972 in lieu of death duties (originally a pendant to the *cassone* now at Chantilly); the striking and monumental *Portrait of Sigismondo Malatesta* by Piero della Francesca (p 144), one of the great masters whose absence from the Louvre had long been deplored; and, finally, the *Madonna* by Marco Zoppo.

CENNI DI PEPE, called CIMABUE
Florence, *circa* 1240—Florence, after 1302
Maesta; the Madonna and Child in Majesty
surrounded by angels, circa 1270 (?)
Wood 427 × 280 cm
From the Church of San Francesco, Pisa
Entered in 1814

GIOTTO DI BONDONE
Colle di Vespignano, *circa* 1267—Florence,
1337
St Francis of Assisi receiving the Stigmata
Predella: *The Vision of Pope Innocent III; the
Pope receiving the statutes of the Order; St Francis
preaching to the birds, circa* 1295/1300 (?)
Wood 313 × 163 cm
From the Church of San Francesco, Pisa
Entered in 1814

Here Giotto revives some of the compositions illustrating different episodes of the life of St Francis as he had painted them in the mural frescoes of the Basilica at Assisi during the last decade of the thirteenth century. The four scenes form a kind of abridged version of the artist's original creation. Giotto's main innovation was his ability to represent holy figures as human beings and as solid forms arranged in three-dimensional space.

MASTER OF THE ST GEORGE CODEX
Active in Tuscany and at Avignon (?) at
the beginning of the 14th century
*The Virgin and Child on a throne
surrounded by angels; St John the Baptist, St
Peter, and two saints*, between 1320 and 1340
Wood 56 × 21 cm
Purchased in 1828

SIMONE MARTINI
Siena, *circa* 1284—Avignon, 1344
The Carrying of the Cross, circa 1336/42 (?)
Wood 28 × 16 cm
Purchased in 1834

Bolognese painter
Triptych, 1333
Central panel: *The Coronation of the Virgin, The Crucifixion*
Wood 73 × 135 cm
Left wing: *The Angel of the Annunciation, The Madonna of Mercy, Saints Margaret,
Catherine, and Lucy* (?)
Right wing: *The Virgin of the Annunciation, The Nativity, Three Martyr Saints*
Wood 127 × 36 cm (each wing)
Collection of the Marquis Campana, purchased in 1863

PIETRO DA RIMINI
Active in Rimini during the first half of
the 14th century
The Deposition from the Cross, circa 1330/40
Wood 43 × 35 cm
Brauer gift, 1932

LORENZO VENEZIANO
Active in Venice from 1356 to 1372
The Madonna and Child, 1372
Wood 126 × 56 cm
Collection of the Marquis Campana, purchased in 1863

GIOVANNI DA MILANO
Active in Florence between 1320 and 1369
St Francis of Assisi, circa 1360
Wood 113 × 39 cm
Collection of the Marquis Campana, purchased in 1863

GENTILE DA FABRIANO
Fabriano, *circa* 1370—Rome, 1427
The Presentation in the Temple, 1423
Wood 26 × 66 cm
From the church of Santa Trinita, Florence
Entered in 1814

ANTONIO PISANO, called PISANELLO
Verona (?) before 1395–? 1455 (?)
Portrait assumed to be of Ginevra d'Este, circa 1436–8 (?)
Wood 43 × 30 cm
Purchased in 1893

JACOPO BELLINI
Active in Venice from 1423—Venice, 1470
The Madonna and Child adored by Lionello d'Este, circa 1450
Wood 60 × 40 cm
Purchased in 1873

FRA ANGELICO
Vicchio di Mugello (?), *circa* 1400 (?)—Rome, 1455
The Coronation of the Virgin, circa 1430/5
Wood 209 × 206 cm
Predella: *Five scenes from the life of St Dominic*
Wood 295 × 210 cm
From the church of the Convent of San Domenico, Fiesole
Entered in 1814

FRA ANGELICO
Vicchio di Mugello (?), *circa* 1400 (?)—
Rome, 1455
*The Martyrdom of St Cosmo and St
Damian, circa* 1440
Wood 37 × 46 cm
Purchased *circa* 1882

FILIPPO LIPPI
Florence, *circa* 1406/07—Spoleto, 1469
*The Madonna and Child surrounded by
angels, with St Frediano and St Augustine,
circa* 1437/8
Wood 208 × 244 cm
From the church of Santo Spirito,
Florence
Entered in 1814

PIERO DELLA FRANCESCA
Borgo San Sepolcro, 1422 (?)—Borgo San Sepolcro, 1492
Sigismondo Malatesta, circa 1451
Wood 44 × 34 cm
Purchased in 1978

STEFANO DI GIOVANNI, called SASSETTA
Siena, 1392 (?)—Siena, 1450
The Madonna and Child surrounded by six angels
Wood 207 × 118 cm
St Anthony of Padua
St John the Evangelist
Wood 195 × 57 cm (each wing)
Panels from the altarpiece of San Francesco, Borgo San
Sepolcro (1437/44)
Purchased in 1956

ALESSO BALDOVINETTI
Florence, *circa* 1426—Florence, 1499
The Madonna and Child, circa 1460/5
Wood 106 × 75 cm
Purchased in 1898 with the help of the Société des Amis
du Louvre

PAOLO UCCELLO
Florence, 1397—Florence, 1475
The Battle of San Romano, circa 1450/6
Wood 180 × 316 cm
Collection of the Marquis Campana, purchased in 1863

ANDREA MANTEGNA
Isola di Carturo, *circa* 1430/1—Mantua, 1506
Calvary, between 1457 and 1460
Wood 76 × 96 cm
From the church of San Zeno, Verona
Entered in 1798

This panel once formed the central part of the predella of the great altarpiece painted by Mantegna, then at the height of his powers, for the High Altar of the Church of San Zeno, Verona. In order to represent the drama of the Crucifixion with historical accuracy, Mantegna has attempted a grandiose and archaeologically exact recreation of classical antiquity. The steep perspective through which the rocky landscape is seen is achieved with astonishing virtuosity.

ANDREA MANTEGNA
Isola di Carturo, *circa* 1430/1—Mantua, 1506
St Sebastian, circa 1480
Canvas 255 × 140 cm
Purchased in 1960

ANDREA MANTEGNA
Isola di Carturo, *circa* 1430/1—Mantua, 1506
Wisdom triumphant over the Vices, circa 1502
Canvas 160 × 92 cm
From the collection of Isabella d'Este at Mantua, collection of the
Duc de Richelieu
Entered in 1801

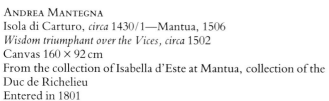

GIOVANNI BELLINI
Venice, *circa* 1430—Venice, 1516
Calvary, circa 1465/70
Wood 70 × 63 cm
Purchased in 1970

ANTONELLO DA MESSINA
Messina, *circa* 1430—Messina, 1479
Portrait of a man,
called *'Il Condottiere',* 1475
Wood 35 × 28 cm
Purchased in 1865

COSIMO TURA
Known in Ferrara from 1431 to 1495
The Pietà, circa 1480
Wood 132 × 268 cm
Collection of the Marquis Campana, purchased in 1863

GIOVANNI BELLINI
Venice, *circa* 1430—Venice, 1516
Christ's Blessing, circa 1460
Wood 58 × 46 cm
Purchased in 1912

Alessandro di Mariano Filipepi, called Sandro Botticelli
Florence, 1445—Florence, 1510
Venus and the Graces offering gifts to a young girl, circa 1430/3
Fresco 212 × 284 cm (detail above)
Purchased in 1882

This fresco, with its companion piece also in the Louvre, once decorated the loggia of a villa near Florence. It represents a young man before an allegorical gathering of the Liberal Arts, and the exact interpretation of the subjects and the identification of the young woman receiving gifts from Venus and the Graces have given rise to various hypotheses. The dancing rhythm and light elegance are close to the Uffizzi's *Primavera,* and the work also reflects the ideas on Love prevalent in Florence in the circle of Neo-Platonic humanists which was grouped around Marsilio Ficino and Lorenzo the Magnificent.

FILIPPINO LIPPI
Prato (?), 1457 (?)—Florence, 1504
The swooning of Esther before Ahasuerus,
circa 1475
Wood 48 × 132 cm
Purchased in 1972

DOMENICO GHIRLANDAIO
Florence, 1449—Florence, 1494
Portrait of an old man and a young boy, circa 1488
Wood 63 × 46 cm
Purchased in 1886

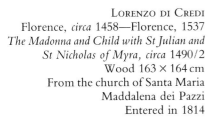

LORENZO DI CREDI
Florence, *circa* 1458—Florence, 1537
The Madonna and Child with St Julian and
St Nicholas of Myra, circa 1490/2
Wood 163 × 164 cm
From the church of Santa Maria
Maddalena dei Pazzi
Entered in 1814

CIMA DA CONEGLIANO
Conegliano, 1459/60—Conegliano (?), 1517/18
The Madonna and Child with St John the Baptist and Mary Magdalen, circa 1510/15
Wood 167 × 110 cm
From the church of the Convent of San Domenico, Parma

VITTORE CARPACCIO
Venice, *circa* 1460/5—Venice, 1525/6
The sermon of St Stephen at Jerusalem, 1514 (?)
Canvas 148 × 194 cm
Entered in 1814

CARLO BRACCESCO
Known in Liguria and in Lombardy from 1478 to 1501
Triptych, circa 1480/1500
Central panel: *The Annunciation*
Wood 158 × 107 cm

Left wing: *St Benedict and St Augustine*
Right wing: *St Stephen and St Ange*
Wood 105 × 52 cm (each wing)
Purchased in 1812

The sixteenth century in Italy

The collection of Italian High Renaissance paintings undoubtedly constitutes one of the most irreplaceable treasures of the Louvre; there is hardly a single comparable public collection outside Italy. Its foundations were laid by François I, who set out deliberately to invite to France the most 'modern' artists of the time, the Italian masters. He composed a marvellous gallery of their works, assembled as an example to others and for his own glory as much as for his personal enjoyment. We know that in 1516 he succeeded in attracting the most famous of these artists, Leonardo da Vinci (of whom Louis XII had already been a patron), and in re-uniting several of his rare paintings: the *Mona Lisa* (p 155), the *Madonna of the rocks*, already in the collection of Louis XII (p 157), '*La Belle Ferronnière*', and the *Virgin and Child with St Anne* (p 156), as well as his *St John the Baptist* (p 157), which later had to leave the royal collections but was returned in the seventeenth century. He acquired the works of other Florentine artists such as Fra Bartolommeo and Andrea del Sarto (who painted *Charity* during a stay in France in 1518), and he employed Rosso Fiorentino for the decoration of Fontainebleau. It was for François I that Raphael painted *St Michael confounding the Devil* (p 162) in 1518, as well as the great *Holy Family*, and that Sebastiano del Piombo painted the *Visitation* (p 166) in 1521. Among other paintings of importance collected by the King (apart from Leonardo and Michelangelo's paintings of *Leda*, both mysteriously lost) were '*La Belle Jardinière*' (p 159) and the *Portrait of the artist with a friend* by Raphael, Giulio Romano's *Joanna of Aragon*, and Savoldo's presumed *Self portrait*. The King also commissioned his portrait in profile from Titian, painted in 1538 after Benvenuto Cellini's medallion.

This basic heritage, kept for a long time at the Château de Fontainebleau and later transferred to the Louvre, was to be considerably enriched when Louis XIV in turn undertook to form a collection whose opulence would illustrate and mirror the brilliance of his reign. The acquisition of part of Cardinal Mazarin's collection in 1661 and of that of the banker Everhard Jabach in 1662–71 brought many superb pictures into the collection. These included Correggio's *Antiope* (p 161), the *St Catherine* (p 162) and the *Allegories* from Isabella d'Este's *studiolo*; the *Portrait of Balthasar Castiglione* (p 160), the small *St George* (p 158) and the *St Michael* by Raphael; the '*Concert champêtre*' (p 164) and several other paintings by Titian, notably the *Pardo Venus*, *The Entombment* (p 165), the *Supper at Emmaus*, and *The Man with a glove* (p 164); as well as paintings by Veronese and Giulio Romano. Many of these paintings had been bought in London in about 1650 when Charles I's famous collection was dispersed. The King's collection had been, undoubtedly, the finest in Europe at the beginning of the seventeenth century, some of the Italian paintings having come from the Gonzaga family collection in Mantua which Charles I had purchased, almost in its entirety, in 1627.

Other Italian Renaissance paintings were soon introduced to Louis XIV's collection: works by Bronzino, Lotto (p 167), Pontormo, Palma Vecchio (p 166); a series of paintings by Jacopo Bassano which were to decorate one of the rooms of the Grands Appartements at Versailles, but which unfortunately included none of his masterpieces; and more paintings by

Veronese (p 168), including the vast and superb *Feast at the House of Simon*, offered to the King by the Republic of Venice. During the reign of Louis XV this last painting was incorporated in the decoration of the Salon d'Hercule at Versailles, designed by the architect Robert de Cotte. There were few acquisitions of Italian Renaissance masters under Louis XV and Louis XVI. In 1741 Hyacinthe Rigaud was amongst those who advised the purchase of the *Madonna with a veil* by Raphael and the *Madonna with the green cushion* by Solario (p 157) from the estate of the Prince de Carignan. When d'Angiviller set up his policy of systematic acquisitions with a view to perfecting the King's collection and making it a public museum, he preferred, quite reasonably, to concentrate on schools and periods of art which were less well represented than those of the Italian Renaissance.

The influx of the paintings seized in Italy during the Revolution and the Empire must have made the Louvre into a real 'wonderland' of the Italian Renaissance; but it was to be a fleeting dream. In 1815 representatives from the allied countries took back all the masterpieces from Rome and Florence, and from Parma, Venice, and Bologna, leaving only a handful: the *Paradise* by Tintoretto (p 168), the *Holy Family* by Pontormo (p 163), the *Crowning with thorns* by Titian (p 166), and the *Circumcision* by Barocci (p 170), which was left at Notre Dame and not returned to the Louvre until 1862. Also left, in exchange for Le Brun's *Feast in the House of Simon*, was the vast *Marriage at Cana* by Veronese (p 169). Among the Italian Renaissance works which entered the Louvre during the Revolution and which remained there, were pictures from France itself: works by Mantegna, Costa, and Perugino from Isabella d'Este's collection, seized in 1801 from the Château de Richelieu; the *Mystic marriage of St Catherine* by Bartolommeo (p 158) from the cathedral of Autun; his *Incredulity of St Thomas* from the Chapelle des Florentins at Lyon; and the *Pietà* by Rosso Fiorentino (p 163) seized from the chapel of the Château d'Ecouen.

Among the acquisitions of the nineteenth century, albeit few in an area already so rich, Lotto's *St Jerome* (p 167), purchased in 1857, was important, as were the sacred and profane frescoes by Bernardino Luini, acquired in 1853 and 1867 from the Villa Pelucca and the Palazzo Litti. These frescoes completed the collection of paintings by Luini, who was much appreciated by many nineteenth-century art lovers for the languid delicacy of his art. Works by other Lombard painters of the beginning of the sixteenth century were also acquired.

Rich as it may be, the Louvre's collection of Cinquecento paintings obviously has gaps. We have once again acquired a taste for Mannerist art, but it is less well represented in the Museum than the classicism of the Renaissance, which has proved consistently more popular with French connoisseurs. It is surely significant that the only painting by Parmigianino (an artist well represented, admittedly, in the Cabinet des Dessins) should have had its unusual design radically altered, by enlarging the painting and balancing the composition, in order to try to justify an attribution to Raphael. The most recent purchases of sixteenth-century works—and we naturally hope that there will be more—have taken into account the need to illustrate better the different cross-currents of the Italian Mannerists. The Tuscan origin of the movement is shown by Beccafumi's *predella*, purchased in 1966, the diffusion of the style in Fontainebleau by *Landscape with the rape of Proserpina* by Niccolo dell'Abbate (p 163), bought in 1933, and the movement at Prague by Arcimboldo's *Seasons*, bought in 1964.

LEONARDO DA VINCI
Vinci, 1452—Cloux, 1519
'La Gioconda', called Mona Lisa, circa 1503/06
Wood 77 × 53 cm
Collection of François I

LEONARDO DA VINCI
Vinci, 1452—Cloux, 1519
The Virgin and Child with St Anne, circa 1508/10
168 × 130 cm
Collection of François I, collection of Louis XIII

The cartoon in the National Gallery, London and several other drawings are preliminary stages in the creation of this unfinished composition, which is one of the last surviving works of Leonardo. The vast landscape of mountains blurred in the haze conveys, as does that of the *Mona Lisa*, Leonardo's cosmic vision of nature. The rhythmic arrangement of the figures, linked by a touching and mysterious feeling of tenderness, reflects his unceasing quest for harmony and balance.

LEONARDO DA VINCI
Vinci, 1452—Cloux, 1519
St John the Baptist, circa 1513/15 (?)
Wood 69 × 57 cm
Collection of François I

LEONARDO DA VINCI
Vinci, 1452—Cloux, 1519
The Madonna of the rocks, 1483 (?)
Wood transferred to canvas 199 × 122 cm
Collection of Louis XII (?)

ANDREA SOLARIO
Milan, *circa* 1470/5—Milan or Pavia, 1524
The Madonna of the green cushion, circa 1507/10
Wood 60 × 47 cm
Collection of Louis XV, purchased in 1742

RAFFAELLO SANZIO, called RAPHAEL
Urbino, 1483—Rome, 1520
St George, circa 1505
Wood 32 × 27 cm
Collection of Louis XIV, purchased in 1661

PIETRO PERUGINO
Città della Pieve, *circa* 1448—Fontignano, 1523
Apollo and Marsyas, circa 1495
Wood 39 × 29 cm
Purchased in 1883

FRA BARTOLOMMEO
Florence, 1475—Florence, 1517
The Mystic marriage of St Catherine, 1511
Wood 257 × 228 cm
From the collegiate church of Notre Dame,
Autun
Entered in 1800

158

RAFFAELLO SANZIO, called RAPHAEL
Urbino, 1483—Rome, 1520
*'La Belle Jardinière', The Virgin and Child with St John the
Baptist*, 1507
Wood 122 × 80 cm
Collection of François I (?)

Popularised by its vivid title, this Virgin and Child with the
young St John in a meadow dates from Raphael's Florentine
period and is a mature work inspired by Leonardo and
Michelangelo. During this time the artist painted several
variations on the same theme, for example, *The Madonna of the
Belvedere* now in Vienna and *The Madonna of the goldfinch* in
Florence, always basing his design on the perfect balance of a
pyramid.

RAFFAELLO SANZIO, called RAPHAEL
Urbino, 1483—Rome, 1520
Balthasar Castiglione, circa 1514/15
Canvas 82 × 67 cm
Collection of Louis XIV, purchased in 1661

ANTONIO ALLEGRI, called CORREGGIO
Correggio, 1489—Correggio, 1534
Venus, Satyr, and Cupid, erroneously called *The Sleep of Antiope*, 1524/5
Canvas 190 × 124 cm
Collection of Louis XIV

ANTONIO ALLEGRI, called CORREGGIO
Correggio, 1489—Correggio, 1534
The Mystic marriage of St Catherine, circa 1526/7
Wood 105 × 102 cm
Collection of Louis XIV

RAFFAELLO SANZIO, called RAPHAEL
Urbino, 1483—Rome, 1520
St Michael confounding the Devil, 1518
Wood transferred to canvas 268 × 160 cm
Collection of François I

ANDREA DEL SARTO
Florence, 1486—Florence, 1530
The Holy Family, circa 1515/16
Wood 141 × 106 cm
Collection of François I

GIACOMO CARUCCI, called PONTORMO
Pontormo, 1494—Florence, 1556
The Holy Family, circa 1527/9
Wood 228 × 176 cm
From the Convent of St Anna at Verzaia, Florence
Entered in 1814

NICCOLÒ DELL' ABBATE
Modena, *circa* 1509 or 1512—Fontainebleau or Paris, 1571 (?)
The rape of Proserpina, circa 1560
Canvas 196 × 218 cm
Purchased in 1933

GIOVANNI BATTISTA DI JACOPO, called
ROSSO FIORENTINO
Florence, 1495—Fontainebleau, 1540
Pietà, circa 1530/5
Wood transferred to canvas
125 × 159 cm
Seized during the French Revolution
(collection of Louis-Joseph de Bourbon,
Prince de Condé)

Tiziano Vecellio, called Titian
Pieve di Cadore, 1488/9—Venice, 1576
Portrait of a man, called *The man with a glove, circa* 1520/3
Canvas 100 × 89 cm
Collection of Louis XIV, purchased in 1671

Tiziano Vecellio, called Titian
Pieve di Cadore, 1488/9—Venice, 1576
'Le concert champêtre', circa 1510/11
Canvas 110 × 138 cm
Collection of Louis XIV, purchased in 1671

TIZIANO VECELLIO, called TITIAN
Pieve di Cadore, 1488/9—Venice, 1576
The Entombment, circa 1525
Canvas 148 × 205 cm
Collection of Louis XIV, purchased in 1662

This painting was executed in about 1525 for the Gonzagas of
Mantua and is one of Titian's supreme classical masterpieces,
probably inspired by Raphael's *Deposition*. Based on a
masterly play of expressive contrasts, notably in the contrast
of light and shadow to convey twilight, the composition is an
example of the lyrical Venetian Grand Manner and has always
been admired and emulated.

JACOMO PALMA VECCHIO
Serimalta, *circa* 1480—Venice, 1528
The Adoration of the Shepherds, circa 1515/20
Canvas 140 × 210 cm
Collection of Louis XIV, purchased in
1685

SEBASTIANO DEL PIOMBO
Venice (?), *circa* 1485—Rome, 1547
The Visitation, 1521
Canvas 168 × 132 cm
Collection of François I

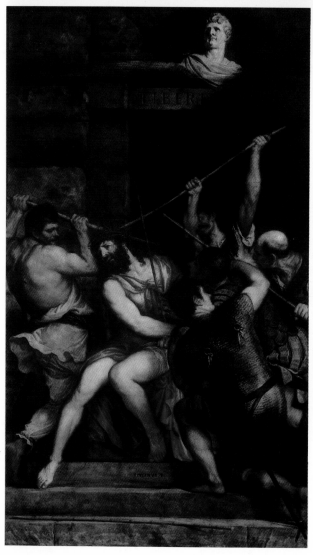

TIZIANO VECELLIO, called TITIAN
Pieve di Cadore, 1488/9—Venice, 1576
The Crowning with thorns, circa 1542
Wood 303 × 180 cm
From Santa Maria delle Grazie, Milan
Entered in 1797

Giovanni Girolamo Savoldo
Brescia, *circa* 1480/5—Venice (?), after 1548
Self portrait, formerly called *Portrait of Gaston de Foix*, *circa* 1531/2
Canvas 91 × 23 cm
Collection of François I (?)

Lorenzo Lotto
Venice, 1480—Loretto, 1556
St Jerome in the desert, 1506
Wood 48 × 40 cm
Purchased in 1857

Lorenzo Lotto
Venice, 1480—Loretto, 1556
Christ and the woman taken in adultery, *circa* 1530/5
Canvas 124 × 156 cm
Collection of Louis XIV

JACOPO ROBUSTI, called TINTORETTO
Venice, 1512—Venice, 1594
Paradise, circa 1578/9
Canvas 143 × 362 cm
Sketch for the *Paradise* of the Great Council Room
of the Palazzo Ducale in Venice
From the Palazzo Bevilacqua, Verona
Entered in 1799

PAOLO CALIARI, called VERONESE
Verona, 1528—Venice, 1588
The Supper at Emmaus, circa 1559/60
Canvas 290 × 448 cm
Collection of Louis XIV

PAOLO CALIARI, called VERONESE
Verona, 1528—Venice, 1588
The Marriage at Cana, 1562/3
Canvas 666 × 990 cm
From the Convent of San Giorgio Maggiore, Venice
Entered in 1798

This picture was painted for the refectory of the Benedictine
convent on the Isola di San Giorgio Maggiore, Venice, built
by Palladio. Veronese designed the vast canvas as though it
were a stage set. In an airy architectural setting inspired by
Palladio, he transforms the Biblical scene into a splendid and
fashionable wedding feast whose guests include, according to
legend, the great princes of the time, François I, Charles V, and
Suleiman the Magnificent (on the left). The musicians in the
centre are said to be portraits of contemporary artists: Titian,
Tintoretto, Bassano, Palladio, and Veronese himself.

FEDERICO BAROCCI
Urbino, *circa* 1535—Urbino, 1612
The Circumcision, 1590
Canvas 374 × 252 cm
From the Church of the Brotherhood of the Name of Jesus at
Pesaro
Entered in 1798

The fifteenth and sixteenth centuries in Flanders and Holland

It is very probable that the collection of François I originally contained paintings by contemporary Flemish artists. We know that the Antwerp artist Joos van Cleve, who came to Fontainebleau in about 1530, painted portraits of the King and members of his family, but not one remained in the royal collections, although they are known by various copies in several museums.

When Le Brun drew up an inventory of the King's collection in 1683 he recorded three or four Flemish paintings of the fifteenth and early sixteenth centuries: The *Wedding at Cana* by Gerard David (p 179), then attributed to Jean de Bruges; and, under the name of Holbein, both the *Sacrifice of Abraham*, now attributed to the Brunswick Monogrammist, and the *Portrait of a man* by Joos van Cleve. The paintings by early Flemish masters at the Musée Napoléon included several panels of van Eyck's *Altarpiece of the Mystic Lamb*, taken from Ghent, and the *Virgin of Canon van der Paele*, taken from Bruges, as well as Memling's triptych of *The Last Judgement* from Danzig and the *St Christopher* triptych from Brussels. All these works were returned to their towns of origin in 1816. *The Annunciation* by Rogier van der Weyden (p 174), which came from Turin, and the *Madonna of Chancellor Rolin* by Jan van Eyck (p 173), from the collegiate church at Autun, have remained in the Louvre. These works excited the curiosity and admiration of young devotees of a return to the Gothic style of painting, like the German philosopher Schlegel and the Boisserée brothers in Cologne, who were to build up a remarkable collection of Flemish and German primitives, now in the Alte Pinakothek at Munich. But the enthusiasm was not yet widespread. Stendhal, faithful to the classical taste for the ideal, if bland, harmonies of the Roman and Bolognese schools, reacted to the popular success of Memling's *Last Judgement* by writing in 1814: 'It's a German School daub . . . people love to see the grimaces of the damned'. Experts and historians are still confused in their knowledge of this School of painting: van der Weyden's *Annunciation*, like Memling's *Last Judgement*, is sometimes regarded as a German work.

Another notable acquisition of the Musée Napoléon was the purchase in Paris in 1806 of *The banker and his wife* signed by Quentin Metsys (p 179). The Restoration and the July Monarchy provided this and many other areas of the collection with few important treasures, although in 1822 '*The pastoral sermon*' (with the church of St Gudule, Brussels, in the background, which gave its name to the artist) was acquired (p 176). On the other hand, the period 1845–1914 saw an uninterrupted series of gifts and purchases. The *Carondolet diptych* by Jan Gossaert (p 180), for instance, was bought in 1847. Memling is exceptionally well represented in the Louvre, thanks chiefly to the bequest by the Comtesse Duchâtel of the great *Virgin and Child with Jacob Floreins* in 1878 and to the purchase of the *Triptych of the Resurrection* (p 176) in 1860 and the *Portrait of an old woman* (p 176) in 1908. At the same time the Flemish primitives section was gaining some measure of consistency with the entry of several works by Dieric Bouts, for example, *The Lamentation* (p 175), and of paintings by

Gerard David, such as the *Sedano triptych*, purchased in 1890, and by Quentin Metsys, Joos van Cleve, Gossaert, Provost, and Bernard van Orley. Works by the Antwerp Mannerists, for example, *Lot and his daughters*, for a long time attributed to Lucas van Leyden (p 181), and the *Martyrdom of St John* from the Schlichting bequest (p 181) in 1914, also supplemented the section. It was at this time that these artists were triumphantly reinstated by a great exhibition in Bruges in 1902, and that their rarity on the market made competition between major museums particularly keen. The keepers of the Louvre succeeded in buying *The Raising of Lazarus* by Geertgen tot Sint Jans (p 177) and a remarkable work by Rogier van der Weyden, the *Braque triptych* in 1913, but they failed in their attempt to secure a work by Hugo van der Goes, the one great master absent from the collections. There is a story that when his admirable *Adoration of the Magi* was discreetly put up for sale by the monastery of Monforte in Spain in 1914 the envoy of the all-powerful Kaiser Friedrich Museum in Berlin arrived a profitable few days before the agents of the Louvre and acquired the painting.

Since then, paintings by artists previously unrepresented have been acquired for the collection. *The Ship of Fools* by Hieronymus Bosch (p 178) was given in 1918 by Camille Benoit, former keeper of the Louvre; the *Christ and the Samaritan woman* by Juan de Flandes (p 178), was bought in 1926 and joined forty years later by another small companion panel of the *Coronation of the Virgin* (p 178), painted for Queen Isabella by Michel Sittow; *St Jerome* by Joachim Patenier (p 180) was given by the English dealer Duveen in 1923; the *Pietà* by Petrus Christus was bought in 1951; and *The fortune teller* by Lucas van Leyden came with the Lebaudy bequest in 1962 (p 181). Christian Aulanier's gift in 1973 of the rare *Christian allegory* by Jan Provost (p 179) should also be recorded.

Different criteria were applied for the introduction to the collection of Dutch painters of the second half of the sixteenth century. The paintings of Lambert Sustris—*Venus and Cupid* (p 184) and *The Baptism of the eunuch*—were in Louis XIV's collection and were appreciated for their affinity to the prestigious Venetian School, whilst the numerous landscapes by Paul Bril were seen as a link with the ideal classical landscapes of Claude and Poussin which he had inspired. The Cabinet du Roi also included Antonio Moro's *Cardinal Granvella's dwarf* (p 183), but the greatest Flemish painter of the century, Pieter Brueghel, was not represented in the Louvre until 1892, when Paul Mantz presented the small but extraordinary *The beggars* (p 182). Other artistic trends of this period were not appreciated by contemporaries, or indeed subsequently until recently. When the Duc de Morny gave Jan Massy's *Bathsheba* (p 184) to the Louvre in 1852 he was accused of ridding himself of a 'complete mediocrity'. It is only thanks to odd donations such as that of Cornelis van Dalem's *Farmyard* (Benoit gift, 1918) and judicious purchases such as *The Artist painting with his family* by Otto van Veen, bought in 1835, and *Justice* by Bartholomeus Spranger, bought in 1936, that artistic currents of the late sixteenth century such as Flemish Mannerism are represented in the Louvre at all.

JAN VAN EYCK
Maaseyck, (?)—Bruges, 1441
The Madonna of Chancellor Rolin, circa 1435
Wood 66 × 62 cm
From the collegiate church of Notre Dame d'Autun
Entered in 1800

This painting shows Nicolas Rolin, Chancellor of Burgundy, kneeling before the Virgin Mary. Chancellor Rolin was an important figure at the court of Philip the Good, who ruled over Burgundy and Flanders. The minutely detailed landscape extending beyond the Romanesque arcade is a composite of various different places. Van Eyck's analytical record of the outward appearance of the world is perfectly unified and the whole painting is charged with an incomparable spiritual intensity.

ROGIER VAN DER WEYDEN
Tournai, 1399/1400—Brussels, 1464
The Annunciation, circa 1435
Wood 86 × 93 cm
From the Royal Gallery, Turin
Entered in 1799

ROGIER VAN DER WEYDEN
Tournai, 1399/1400—Brussels, 1464
Braque family triptych, circa 1450

Central wing: *Christ between the Virgin Mary and St John the Evangelist*
Wood 41 × 68 cm
Left wing: *St John the Baptist*
Right wing: *St Mary Magdalen*
Wood 41 × 34 cm (each wing)
Purchased in 1913

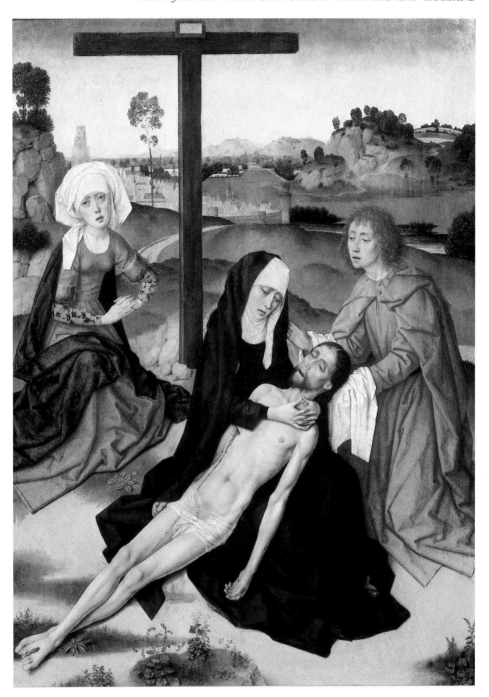

DIERIC BOUTS
Haarlem, *circa* 1420—Louvain, 1475
The Lamentation of Christ, circa 1460
Wood 69 × 49 cm
Bequeathed by M. Mongé-Misbach, 1871

MASTER OF THE VIEW OF ST GUDULE
Active in Brussels between 1470 and 1490
The preaching of St Géry, called *'The pastoral sermon'*, with the church of St Gudule, Brussels, in the background, *circa* 1475/80
Wood 98 × 69 cm
Purchased in 1922

HANS MEMLING
Seligenstadt am Main, *circa* 1435— Bruges, 1494
Portrait of an old woman, circa 1470/5
Wood 35 × 29 cm
Purchased in 1908

HANS MEMLING
Seligenstadt am Main, *circa* 1435—Bruges, 1494
Triptych of the Resurrection, circa 1490
Central panel: 61 × 44 cm
Left wing: *The Martyrdom of St Sebastian*
Right wing: *The Ascension*
Wood 61 × 18 cm (each wing)
Purchased in 1860

GEERTGEN TOT SINT JANS
Leiden (?), 1460/5—Haarlem, 1488/93
The Raising of Lazarus, circa 1480
Wood 127 × 97 cm
Purchased in 1902

MICHEL SITTOW
Reval, *circa* 1468—Reval, 1525/6
The Coronation of the Virgin, between 1496 and 1504
Wood 24 × 18 cm
Purchased in 1966

HIERONYMUS BOSCH
Bois-le-Duc, *circa* 1450—Bois-le-Duc, 1516
The Ship of Fools, circa 1500 (?)
Wood 58 × 32 cm
Presented by Camille Benoit, 1918

JUAN DE FLANDES
Known in Castille from 1496—Palencia, 1519
Christ and the Samaritan woman, between 1496 and 1504
Wood 24 × 17 cm
Purchased in 1926

QUENTIN METSYS
Louvain, 1465/6—Antwerp, 1530
The banker and his wife, 1514
Wood 70 × 67 cm
Purchased in 1806

JAN PROVOST
Mons, *circa* 1465—Bruges, 1529
Christian allegory, *circa* 1500/10
Wood 50 × 40 cm
Presented by Christiane Aulanier, 1973

GERARD DAVID
Ouwater, 1450/60—Brúges, 1523
The marriage at Cana, *circa* 1500
Wood 100 × 128 cm
Collection of Louis XIV, entered before 1683

JOACHIM PATENIER
Dinant, *circa* 1480—Antwerp, 1524
St Jerome in the desert, circa 1515 (?)
Wood 78 × 37 cm
Presented by Sir Joseph Duveen, 1923

JAN GOSSAERT, called MABUSE
Maubeuge (?), *circa* 1478—Middelburg, 1532
Carondolet diptych, 1517
Left wing: *Jean Carondolet*
Right wing: *Virgin and Child*
Curved wood 42 × 27 cm (each wing)
Purchased in 1847

JOOS VAN CLEVE
Cleves (?), *circa* 1485—Antwerp, 1540/1
The Lamentation of Christ, circa 1530
Wood 145 × 204 cm
Central panel of an altarpiece which includes a lunette
(*The Stigmatization of St Francis*) and a predella (*The
Last Supper*)
From the church of Santa Maria della Pace, Genoa
Entered in 1813

LUCAS VAN LEYDEN
Leiden, 1494—Leiden, 1533
The fortune teller, circa 1510
Wood 24 × 30 cm
Bequeathed by Madame Pierre Lebaudy, 1962

MASTER OF THE MARTYRDOM OF ST JOHN
Active in Antwerp, *circa* 1525
The Martyrdom of St John the Evangelist, circa 1525
Curved wood 117 × 67 cm
Bequeathed by Baron Basil de Schlichting, 1914

Anonymous artist of Antwerp or Leiden
First half of the 16th century
Lot and his daughters, circa 1520
Wood 48 × 34 cm
Purchased in 1900
Previously attributed to Lucas van Leyden

PIETER BRUEGEL THE ELDER
Brueghel (?), *circa* 1525—Brussels, 1569
The beggars, 1568
Wood 18 × 21 cm
Presented by Paul Mantz, 1892

Although small in scale, this work concisely expresses Bruegel's sarcastic, anguished, but ultimately sympathetic view of the human condition. It has been suggested both that he is depicting a simple scene of the departure of the lepers of Lazaretto for a carnival, and that the cripples have a political, sociological, or moral significance, but in either case the artist gives a powerful impression of the physical misery and the moral isolation of these outcasts.

CORNELIS VAN DALEM
Known in Antwerp between 1545 and 1573/6
Farmyard with a beggar, circa 1560 (?)
Wood 38 × 53 cm
Presented by Camille Benoit, 1918

ANTHONIS MOR VAN DASHORST, called
ANTONIO MORO
Utrecht, 1519—Antwerp, 1575
Cardinal Granvella's dwarf, circa 1560
Wood 126 × 92 cm
Collection of Louis XIV, entered before
1683

JAN MASSYS
Antwerp, *circa* 1509—Antwerp, *circa* 1575
David and Bathsheba, 1562
Wood 162 × 197 cm
Presented by the Comte du Morny, 1852

LAMBERT SUSTRIS
Amsterdam, between 1515 and 1520—Padua (?), after 1568
Venus and Cupid, circa 1560 (?)
Canvas 132 × 184 cm
Collection of Louis XIV, entered before 1683

The seventeenth century in Flanders

The first Flemish paintings to enter the royal collection in the seventeenth century were by living artists who had been brought to work in Paris by Marie de Médicis. Frans Pourbus painted the Queen's official portrait for the Petite Galerie of the Louvre and some large religious canvases for churches, including *The Last Supper*, which was seized during the Revolution. Rubens, the famous Antwerp master, was commissioned by the Queen Mother to paint the decorations for the Long Gallery of the Palais du Luxembourg, inaugurated in 1625 for the marriage of Henrietta of France with Charles I of England. It consisted of twenty-four canvases illustrating and, of course, glorifying episodes in the life of the Queen from her birth in Florence to her reconciliation with her son Louis XIII. Historical facts, both real and slightly imaginary, are mingled with allegory in a vast sensual display, which represents the very summit of Baroque painting. Yet at the time it seems to have struck few chords, as the Parisian taste of the mid-century was attuned to Italian classicism and its sober French interpretation.

It was not until the decade 1660–70 that Flemish paintings entered the royal collections once again. Although they were unimportant in Mazarin's collection, acquired in 1661, the Flemish paintings from the Jabach collection are excellent and include masterpieces by Rubens (*Thomyris and Cyrus* and *The Virgin and innocent saints*) and by van Dyck (the *Palatine Princes*). In Parisian artistic circles battle had already been joined between the partisans of colour, the Rubénistes, and the Poussinistes, who upheld, in the name of classicism, the merits of strict draughtsmanship. Roger de Piles brought the qualities of Rubens to light and the Médicis galleries found new admirers. Collections of Flemish paintings multiplied and the royal collection was enriched with new paintings by van Dyck, the *Virgin with donors* (p 190) and *Venus and Vulcan* (p 190), and by Rubens, including *The kermis* (p 189) bought in 1685 from M. de Hauterive, and with many decorative landscapes by Paul Bril (p 187) and Joos de Momper. Jan Brueghel the Elder's masterpiece, the *Battle of Issus* (p 187), was left to Louis XIV by Le Nôtre in 1693. However, the legend that the King, on seeing a painting by Teniers placed in his apartments, exclaimed 'Rid me of these scarecrows' rings true. The craze for the northern genre artists which spread amongst Parisian collectors and was reflected in the work of young French artists was not yet manifest at Versailles, where the 'Grand Manner' of classical art still reigned supreme.

Whilst many private collections, foremost of which was the incomparable collection of the Duc d'Orléans, were begun or developed during the Regency and the reign of Louis XV, the Cabinet du Roi increased very little. At least the few acquisitions were of the highest quality: Rubens' *The flight of Lot*, bought from the estate of the Prince de Carignan (1741), the *Seven works of mercy*, the first important painting by Teniers in the royal collection, the *Calvary* by van Dyck, then attributed to Rubens (from the Jesuit church of Bergues St Winnocq, 1749), and *Christ driving the merchants from the temple* by Jordaens (p 192), given in 1751 by the painter Charles Joseph Natoire.

Flemish painting was a major feature of the Comte d'Angiviller's programme of acquisition. Bought direct from private collectors, from dealers (especially Lebrun), or from public sales, the paintings he assembled formed an intelligent complement to the original collection. They provided a better illustration of genre painting in the works of Craesbeck and Teniers (p 194) and of religious painting on a grand scale by Rubens' *The Martyrdom of St Liévin*, bought at the sale of the church of the Flanders Jesuits and sent to the museum in Brussels in 1803, and his *Adoration of the Magi*. The paintings also improved the representation of Jordaens, *The Four Evangelists* (p 193), of van Dyck, with his *Charles I*, bought in 1775 from Madame du Barry (p 191), and of Rubens the portraitist with *Helena Fourment and her children*, purchased at the comte de Vaudreuil's sale in 1784.

The seizure of treasures from the nobility at the time of the Revolution ensured the acquisition of genre paintings and small format collectors' pieces (Francken, Teniers, Neeffs) and of still lifes (Snyders, Fyt) which were plentiful in Parisian collections. It also claimed large religious and mythological canvases, such as *St Macarius of Ghent* by Jacob van Oost, seized from the Prince de Conti (p 192) and *Hercules and Omphale* by Rubens, which were all that remained when the Galerie d'Orléans was exported wholesale to England. Of the paintings taken from Flanders during the Revolution, including works such as the *Descent from the Cross* or the *'Coup de Lance'* by Rubens, nearly all were returned to their country of origin in 1815. After this dramatic reflux the desolated walls of the Louvre had to be rehung: a noteworthy solution was the return of the Marie de Médicis cycle by Rubens from the Musée du Luxembourg. The Restoration was hardly more favourable to the Flemish Schools than to other sections of the Museum, but two important paintings by Jordaens were bought, *Jupiter fed by the goat Amalthea* and *Portrait of a man*, and later two new paintings by Rubens, his *Portrait of the Baron de Vicq* and a sketch for the Médicis galleries.

On the other hand, the period of the Second Empire was particularly extravagant, as the La Caze donation in 1869 consisted of more than seventy paintings. These included still lifes by Fyt (p 194) and Snyders, a series of paintings by Teniers, paintings by van Dyck such as the *Martyrdom of St Sebastian* and, most important of all, a series of sketches by Rubens, *Philopoemen recognised* (p 189) and sketches for the ceiling of the church of the Antwerp Jesuits. These had been chosen for their dazzling freedom of execution by Dr La Caze, who was an ardent admirer of Watteau and Fragonard.

Most of the Flemish paintings which have entered the Louvre in the last hundred years have done so thanks to private generosity. For instance, *The standard-bearer* by Victor Boucquet (p 192), the *Twilight landscape* by Adriaen Brouwer (p 194), and the great *Ixion tricked by Juno* were part of the Schlichting bequest in 1914. *The death of Dido* by Rubens and the *Portrait of a gentleman* by van Dyck were amongst the very fine paintings given by Carlos de Beistegui in 1942. The van Dyck collection was lacking one of his great portraits of the Genoese aristocracy, and this gap was filled by the gift of a *Portrait of the Marchesa Spinola Doria* in 1949 by Baron Edouard de Rothschild's heirs. Rubens' *Portrait of Helena Fourment with a carriage* (p 190) came from the same collection, in payment of capital transfer tax. Acquired by Baron Alphonse de Rothschild from the Duke of Marlborough in 1884, this masterpiece of European portraiture was one of the most important treasures to enter the Louvre since the Second World War.

PAUL BRIL
Antwerp, 1554—Rome, 1626
The stag hunt, circa 1595/1600 (?)
Canvas 105 × 137 cm
Collection of Louis XIV, entered before 1683

JAN BRUEGHEL THE ELDER, called 'VELVET BRUEGHEL'
Brussels, 1568—Antwerp, 1625
The Battle of Issus, 1602
Wood 86 × 135 cm
Collection of Louis XIV, bequeathed to the King by Le Nôtre, 1693

PETER PAUL RUBENS
Siegen, 1577—Antwerp, 1640
The Apotheosis of Henri IV and the proclamation of the regency of
Marie de Médicis on 14 May 1610, circa 1622/4
Canvas 394 × 727 cm
Collection of Louis XIV, entered in 1693

This painting originally occupied the focal point at the end of
the Gallery of the cycle of historical episodes and allegories
painted by Rubens for Marie de Médicis at the Palais du
Luxembourg. It is also central to the theme of the series,
depicting Marie de Médicis assuming the Regency by popular
demand on the death of Henry IV. The large and dynamic
composition, linking the group of the Queen to that of the
King with a double volute, is a powerful example of the
curvilinear rhythms of Baroque art.

PETER PAUL RUBENS
Siegen, 1577—Antwerp, 1640
The kermis, circa 1635
Wood 149 × 261 cm
Collection of Louis XIV, acquired in 1685

PETER PAUL RUBENS
Siegen, 1577—Antwerp, 1640
Philopoemen, General of the Achaeans, recognized by the old woman of Megara,
circa 1610
Wood 50 × 66 cm
Bequeathed by Louis La Caze, 1869

PETER PAUL RUBENS
Siegen, 1577—Antwerp, 1640
Helena Fourment with a carriage, circa 1639
Wood 195 × 132 cm
Acquired in payment of death duties, 1977

ANTHONY VAN DYCK
Antwerp, 1599—Blackfriars, 1641
The Virgin with donors, circa 1627/30
Canvas 250 × 191 cm
Collection of Louis XIV, purchased in 1685

ANTHONY VAN DYCK
Antwerp, 1599—Blackfriars, 1641
Venus asking Vulcan for arms for Aeneas, circa 1630
Canvas 220 × 145 cm
Collection of Louis XIV, purchased between 1684 and 1715

ANTHONY VAN DYCK
Antwerp, 1599—Blackfriars, 1641
Charles I of England out hunting, between 1635 and 1638
Canvas 266 × 207 cm
Collection of Louis XIV, purchased in 1775

As 'Principal Painter in Ordinary' to Charles I, the Flemish
artist van Dyck painted several portraits of the King in armour
or in all his royal splendour. However, he is here shown as a
gentleman returning from the hunt. Van Dyck's image of the
English aristocracy as elegant and yet familiar, with the figure
set in a naturally lit landscape, was to be a prototype for
English portraiture until the nineteenth century.

191

JACOB JORDAENS
Antwerp, 1593—Antwerp, 1678
Christ driving the merchants from the Temple, circa 1650
Canvas 288 × 436 cm
Collection of Louis XV, purchased in 1751

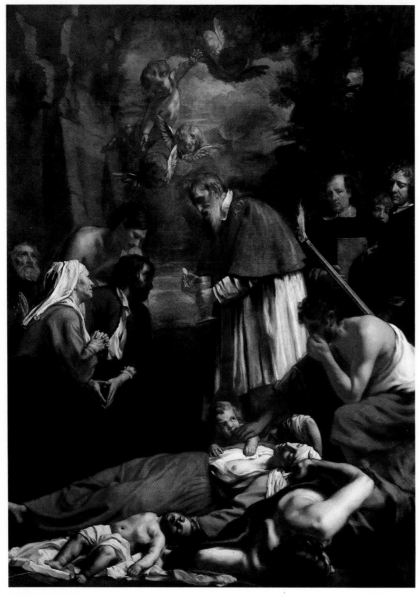

JACOB VAN OOST THE YOUNGER
Bruges, 1637—Bruges, 1713
St Macarius of Ghent giving aid to the plague victims, 1673
Canvas 350 × 257 cm
Seized during the French Revolution (collection of the Prince de Conti)

VICTOR BOUCQUET
Furnes, 1619—Furnes, 1677
The standard-bearer, 1664
Canvas 184 × 112 cm
Presented by the Comtesse de Comminges-Guitaud, 1898

JACOB JORDAENS
Antwerp, 1593—Antwerp, 1678
The Four Evangelists, circa 1625
Canvas 134 × 118 cm
Collection of Louis XVI, purchased in 1784

DAVID TENIERS
Antwerp, 1610—Brussels, 1690
*Heron hunting with the Archduke Leopold
Wilhelm, circa* 1650/60
Canvas 82 × 120 cm
Collection of Louis XVI, purchased in
1784

ADRIAEN BROUWER
Audenarde, 1605/6—Antwerp, 1638
Twilight landscape, circa 1633/7
Wood 17 × 26 cm
Presented by M. Friedsam, 1926

JAN FYT
Antwerp, 1611—Antwerp, 1661
*Game and hunting gear discovered by a cat,
circa* 1640/50 (?)
Canvas 95 × 122 cm
Bequeathed by Louis La Caze, 1869

The seventeenth century in Holland

The pre-eminence accorded to history painting by the Académie Royale de Peinture et de Sculpture placed it at the summit of the hierarchy of acceptable subject matter in seventeenth-century France. Official taste had long been prevented from admiring the contemporary Dutch masters, who painted mainly 'inferior' subjects devoted to the representation of everyday life. Several Dutch Italianate landscapists, such as Jan Asselijn or Herman van Swanevelt, who painted landscapes for the decoration of the Hôtel Lambert (which entered the royal collection under Louis XVI), were appreciated in France at this time, but this was undoubtedly because they were linked to the tradition of ideal classical landscape painting. Rembrandt was not well known in France during his lifetime; people were disconcerted by his technique, 'which often seems nothing but a rough sketch', according to the contemporary architect and critic Félibien des Araux, even when they were not shocked by his 'bad taste'. A diplomatic gift to the King from Maurice of Nassau in 1678/9, the series of *Views of Brazil* by Frans Post, today appreciated for their simple charm, was considered not so much great art, but rather as a document prized for its exoticism, and was duly consigned to the Cabinet des Curiosités. It is not surprising, however, to find among Louis XIV's purchases the great *Still life* by Davidsz de Heem (p 208), a foretaste of the sumptuous decorative displays by Monnoyen and Desportes, and later an inspiration to Matisse, who made two copies.

The first indication of a change of sensibility was the entry into the King's collection in 1671, just two years after the artist's death, of the *Portrait of the artist* of 1660 by Rembrandt. The purchase of several works by Gerard Dou (including *The Bible reading*) between 1684 and 1715 marks a more significant turning-point. From then on French collectors, struck by Flemish painting, also sought landscapes, still lifes, and Dutch genre scenes in which they appreciated the 'truth to life', the delicacy of execution, and the artful light effects. Soon the fashion had spread among a number of young Dutch painters working 'in the style of Rembrandt'. Throughout the eighteenth century it was expressed in the collection of a considerable number of Dutch paintings of the previous century, whose reduced dimensions suited the décor of the smaller rooms then in vogue in France. We should not underestimate the relationship in feeling and pictorial taste which links so many of the great French painters, from Chardin and Oudry to Fragonard and Greuze, to their Dutch predecessors.

In 1742 the royal collection was enriched by the acquisition of several fine paintings from the estate of the Prince de Carignan, including Rembrandt's *The Angel Raphael leaving Tobias*. It was under Louis XVI that the most decisive purchases were made, either through the agency of dealers like Lebrun, who supplied the *Soldier offering money to a woman* by Ter Borch and *The departure for the ride* by Cuyp, or at public sales. At Randon de Boisset's sale in 1777, *The Supper at Emmaus* by Rembrandt (p 200) was bought, and at the Comte de Vaudreuil's sale in 1784 the *Two philosophers* (one now attributed to Samuel Koninck) and the *Portrait of*

Hendrickje Stoffels by Rembrandt, as well as *The Ray of sunlight* by Jacob Ruisdael (p 206), were purchased.

Parisian collectors were quite infatuated with Dutch painting, and there is no better proof of this than the lists of paintings seized from the emigrés. To mention but a few, there are *St Matthew and the Angel* by Rembrandt, his later version of *The Supper at Emmaus* and two self-portraits, the *Adoration of the Shepherds* by Bloemaert (p 197), and *The concert* by Ter Borch. Meanwhile, French painting at the end of the eighteenth century was also affected: Boilly, Marguerite Gérard, and Drolling revived the style of Metsu and Dou, while Demarne and Swebach imitated Wouwerman or Berchem.

Several interesting additions mark the period of the Revolution and the Empire, notably that of the famous *The dropsical woman* by Dou (p 203), given by Charles Emmanuel of Savoy in 1799. From the Stathouder collection, transferred to Paris in 1795, all that remained in 1815 after the allies had retrieved their paintings were *The concert* by Honthorst (p 197) and some pictures by Berchem, Wouwerman, and Weenix.

Appreciation of the Dutch masters in the nineteenth century was found in many quarters. Some of Balzac's descriptions reflect the fervent admiration later expressed by Fromentin in his *Maîtres d'Autrefois* (1876) or the praise of the artists of the Netherlands offered by Théodore Rousseau, Courbet, Manet, and Redon. The second half of the century enjoyed the fruits of this general admiration with a series of purchases or gifts to the Louvre. *The flayed ox* by Rembrandt (p 201) was purchased in 1857, and certain artists who had been ignored for years were represented for the first time. Vermeer, whose reputation had been resuscitated by the French critic Gustave Thoré in 1866 was entered with *The lacemaker* (p 210), and Hobbema was represented with *The water-mill* (p 207). Unfortunately, artists such as Philip Koninck or Jan van de Capelle, who were appreciated by British collectors, did not benefit in this way.

The Dutch paintings of the La Caze bequest in 1869 are, like all those of this infallible connoisseur, of the finest quality. Paintings by Ter Borch, van Ostade, Steen, and van Goyen are dominated by three masterpieces: the incomparable *Bathsheba* by Rembrandt (p 202), and *The gipsy girl* (p 198) and the *Portrait of a woman* by Frans Hals (p 199). Besides important individual donations, international gifts of entire collections at the beginning of this century much increased the Dutch section. The Schlicting bequest in 1914, and particularly the Comte de l'Espine's collection of 1930, which included the mysterious *Pair of slippers* now attributed to Samuel van Hoogstraten, were of the most important of these gifts.

Recent years have proved less prolific. Some purchases or gifts bear witness, albeit insufficient, to the need to represent certain artists and movements. Aert de Gelder, Carel Fabritius, Ter Brugghen (p 197), Coorte, and Sweerts (p 207), and artistic movements such as Mannerism are now represented, and different aspects of an artist's *oeuvre*, such as a *Still life* by Salomon van Ruysdael (p 199), have been brought to the fore again by contemporary historians. Among the donations, three major works stand out: the Rembrandt collection is completed with one of his rare landscapes, *The castle*, presented by M. Nicolas in 1948, and his *Portrait of Titus* and Pieter de Hooch's *A young woman drinking* (p 209), which originally came from the collection of Baron Alphonse de Rothschild, were presented by Mme Piatigorsky in 1974.

GERRIT VAN HONTHORST
Utrecht, 1590—Utrecht, 1656
The concert, 1624
Canvas 168 × 178 cm
From the Stadhouder collection, the Hague
Entered in 1795

ABRAHAM BLOEMAERT
Gorkum, 1564—Utrecht, 1651
Adoration of the Shepherds, 1612
Canvas 287 × 229 cm
From the Milliotty collection
Entered in 1799

HENDRICK TER BRUGGHEN
Deventer, 1588—Utrecht, 1629
The duet, 1628
Canvas 106 × 82 cm
Purchased in 1954

FRANS HALS
Antwerp, *circa* 1581/5—Haarlem, 1666
The gipsy girl, circa 1628/30
Wood 58 × 52 cm
Bequeathed by Louis La Caze, 1869

With this portrait of a jovial gipsy wench, Hals continues in the Caravaggesque tradition of popular subjects which was imported from Rome by Terbrugghen and Honthorst. However, it is the exuberance of the light and colourful brushstrokes of his technique which conveys the sensation of spontaneity and life in this painting. The actual handling of the paint has now become a means of expression in itself.

SALOMON VAN RUYSDAEL
Naarden, 1600/3—Haarlem, 1670
Still life with a turkey, 1661
Canvas 112 × 85 cm
Purchased in 1965

FRANS HALS
Antwerp, *circa* 1581/5—Haarlem, 1666
Portrait of a woman, circa 1650 (?)
Canvas 108 × 80 cm
Bequeathed by Louis La Caze, 1869

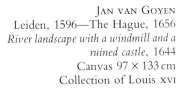

JAN VAN GOYEN
Leiden, 1596—The Hague, 1656
*River landscape with a windmill and a
ruined castle*, 1644
Canvas 97 × 133 cm
Collection of Louis XVI

Harmensz Rembrandt van Rijn
Leiden, 1606—Amsterdam, 1669
The Supper at Emmaus, 1648
Wood 68 × 65 cm
Collection of Louis XVI, purchased in 1777

Rembrandt returned several times to the theme of the Supper
at Emmaus, which explores the double nature of Christ, His
humanity and His essential divinity. Rembrandt interpreted
the theme in a different way each time; the composition of this
version relies on Italian Renaissance examples and is one of the
artist's most serenely classical masterpieces.

HARMENSZ REMBRANDT VAN RIJN
Leiden, 1606—Amsterdam, 1669
Portrait of the artist at his easel, 1660
Canvas 111 × 90 cm
Collection of Louis XIV, purchased in 1671

HARMENSZ REMBRANDT VAN RIJN
Leiden, 1606—Amsterdam, 1669
The flayed ox, 1655
Wood 94 × 69 cm
Purchased in 1857

201

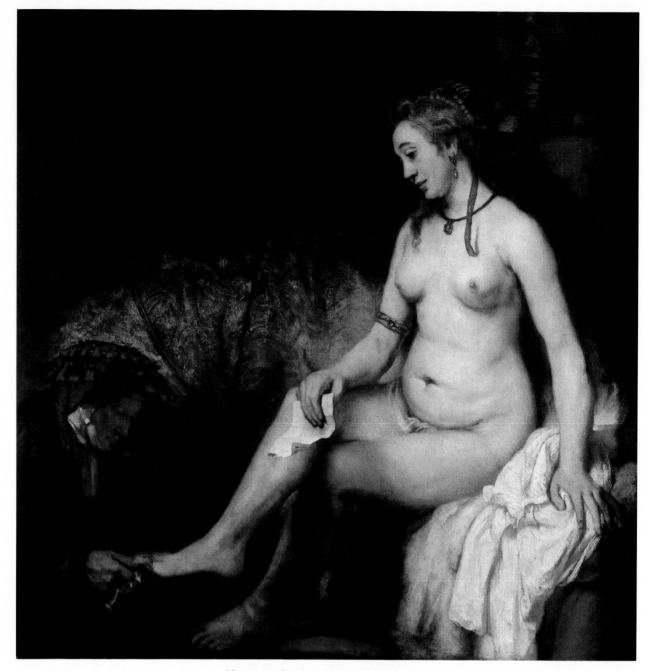

Harmensz Rembrandt van Rijn
Leiden, 1606—Amsterdam, 1669
Bathsheba, 1654
Canvas 142 × 142 cm
Bequeathed by Louis La Caze, 1869

GERARD DOU
Leiden, 1613—Leiden, 1675
The dropsical woman, 1663 (?)
Wood 86 × 67 cm
Presented by Charles Emmanuel IV of Savoy to General
Clauzel for the Louvre, 1799

ADRIAEN VAN OSTADE
Haarlem, 1610—Haarlem, 1685
Portrait of a family, 1654
Wood 70 × 88 cm
Collection of Louis XVI, purchased in 1785

NICOLAES BERCHEM
Haarlem, 1620—Amsterdam, 1683
Landscape with Jacob, Rachel, and Leah,
1643 (?)
Canvas 166 × 138 cm
Purchased in 1816

AELBERT CUYP
Dordrecht, 1620—Dordrecht, 1691
Landscape near Rhenen, circa 1650/5
Canvas 170 × 229 cm
Collection of Louis XVI, purchased in
1783

KAREL DUJARDIN
Amsterdam, 1621/2—Venice, 1678
Italian landscape with herdsmen and a piebald horse, circa 1675 (?)
Wood 32 × 27 cm
Seized during the French Revolution (collection of Baron de Breteuil)

CORNELIS VAN POELENBURGH
Utrecht, *circa* 1586—Utrecht, 1667
Ruins of ancient Rome, circa 1620
Copper 44 × 57 cm
Seized during the French Revolution (Collection of the Duchesse de Noailles)

JAN BAPTIST WEENIX
Amsterdam, 1621—Utrecht, *circa* 1660
Departure of an oriental entourage, circa 1658/60
Canvas 123 × 175 cm
Collection of Louis XVI, purchased in 1783

JACOB RUISDAEL
Haarlem, 1628/9—Amsterdam, 1682
The ray of sunlight, circa 1660 (?)
Canvas 83 × 99 cm
Collection of Louis XVI, purchased in 1784

Apart from the elements borrowed from reality—a windmill, the ruins of Brederode castle, the hills of Guelders, and the banks of the Rhine—Ruisdael's grandiose composition is an imaginary view, a kind of synthesis of the great motifs of Dutch landscape. Even the moving clouds contribute to the strongly architectural construction of the landscape, which is dramatised further by the sharp dissonance of the ray of sunshine.

MICHIEL SWEERTS
Brussels, 1624—Goa, 1664
The young man and the procuress, circa 1660 (?)
Copper 19 × 27 cm
Purchased in 1967

MEINDERT HOBBEMA
Amsterdam, 1638—Amsterdam, 1709
The water-mill, circa 1660/70 (?)
Canvas 80 × 66 cm
Purchased in 1861

JAN VAN DER HEYDEN
Gorkum, 1637—Amsterdam, 1712
*The Dam with the new town hall
at Amsterdam,* 1668
Canvas 73 × 86 cm
Collection of Louis XVI, purchased in 1783

207

Gabriel Metsu
Leiden, 1629—Amsterdam, 1667
The Amsterdam vegetable market
Canvas 97 × 84 cm
Collection of Louis xvi, purchased in 1783

Davidsz de Heem
Utrecht, 1606—Antwerp, 1683/4
A table of desserts, 1640
Canvas 149 × 203 cm
Collection of Louis xiv, purchased before 1683

Gerard ter Borch
Zwolle, 1617—Deventer, 1681
The concert, circa 1657
Wood 47 × 44 cm
Seized during the French Revolution (collection of the Duc de
Brissac)

PIETER DE HOOCH
Rotterdam, 1629—Amsterdam, 1684
A young woman drinking, 1658
Canvas 69 × 60 cm
Presented by Mme Piatigorsky, *née* Rothschild, 1974

This work dates from Pieter de Hooch's best period, 1654–62, when he worked in Delft. During these years he painted tranquil scenes of bourgeois domesticity and conversation pieces set in clearly lit interiors, courtyards, or small gardens. His subtle construction of space in depth and his refined use of lighting create an almost lyrical effect, and his style directly anticipates that of Vermeer.

JAN VERMEER
Delft, 1632—Delft, 1675
The lacemaker, circa 1665
Canvas applied to wood 24 × 21 cm
Purchased in 1870

Spain

At the time of Louis XIV the royal collections contained extremely few Spanish paintings: only *The Burning Bush* by Francisco Collantes (p 218) and the *Portrait of the young Infanta Margarita* by Velasquez (or, according to some critics, his studio). This was the only work of quality among the family portraits with which Queen Anne of Austria, sister of Philip IV, decorated her Cabinet des Bains in the Palais du Louvre. Under Louis XVI some paintings by Murillo, including one of his masterpieces, *The young beggar* (p 220), were purchased from the dealer Lebrun. During the eighteenth century the painters of the Golden Age of Spanish painting had made only a modest impression on the great European collections; only Murillo was really sought after, and this preference was to eclipse the qualities of Velasquez for many years.

During the first half of the nineteenth century a great change in attitude took place, and Spain and Spanish art became fashionable. It was not only the Spain of romance and folklore, with its violent contrasts, which fascinated writers, musicians, and lovers of the 'picturesque' alike, but it was also the Spain of the painters of the Golden Age whose dark and passionate works impressed many young artists of the mid-century who had tired of Romanticism and were anxious to escape the empty rhetoric of the Academy.

The influx of Spanish paintings into France during this period was a manifestation of this Hispanicism. Many important new collections were formed, the earliest being brought back from Spain by various generals at the time of Joseph Bonaparte and the War of Independence. Political circumstances favoured the creation of some collections, such as the famous collection of Maréchal Soult. Later, others were assembled with regular and important purchases, helped, from 1835, by the suppression of the religious orders (L'Esclaustracion) and the rumblings of the Carlist War. Among these was the collection of the financier Aguado, as well as the prodigious Spanish collection of Louis-Philippe, which was created after some intelligent prospecting throughout Spain by Baron Taylor. It contained hundreds of works by all the Spanish masters, with particularly brilliant examples of the art of Zurbaran and Goya, and it was exhibited at the Louvre from 1838–48.

Unfortunately, very few of these paintings remain in the Louvre. The pictures sent from Spain for the Musée Napoléon in 1813 were returned two years later. After the 1848 Revolution the Spanish collection was given back to the Orléans family (although one primitive painting was left, forgotten, in store, only to be recognised in recent years as a work by the Catalan master Huguet). This unique, but short-lived, collection was sold in London in 1853 and is now dispersed in museums all over the world. However, one masterpiece from the Spanish collection has been returned to the Louvre: El Greco's *Christ on the Cross* (p 215), purchased in 1908. Negotiations under Louis-Philippe to buy the collection of Maréchal Soult ended in failure, but the Louvre managed to purchase several very important paintings in 1858 and 1867: *St Basil* by Herrera (p 216), *The angels' kitchen* and *The Birth of the Virgin* (p 219) by Murillo, the two great *Scenes from the life of St Bonaventura* (p 217), and the small *St Apollonia* by

Zurbaran. When part of the collection was sold publicly in 1852, the Louvre managed to buy the famous *Immaculate Conception* by Murillo by raising the bidding to the vast sum of 586,000 francs. In 1940 it went to the Prado as part of an exchange.

In 1865 the first painting by Goya entered the Louvre, his *Portrait of Ferdinand Guillemardet* (p 221), painted when the sitter was French Ambassador in Madrid (1798) and bequeathed by his son. It was the first in a series of his portraits gradually acquired by the Louvre, which undoubtedly has the finest such collection outside Spain, containing *The lady with a fan* (p 221) and *Perez de Castro*, purchased in 1902 and 1858 respectively, the *Marquesa de la Solana* (p 222), justly considered to be one of Goya's finest female portraits and acquired through the generosity of Carlos de Beistegui, and the *Marquesa de Santa Cruz*, recently acquired in lieu of death duties.

During the second half of the nineteenth century and the first years of the twentieth century, the acquisitions of paintings of the Golden Age were less numerous than might have been hoped. However, the *Club-footed boy* by Ribera (p 216) was part of the La Caze donation and El Greco's *St Louis* was acquired in 1903, shortly before his *Christ on the Cross*. None of the paintings which gradually joined Velasquez's *Portrait of the Infanta Margarita*, itself of disputed attribution, can be definitively considered his own. This is a gap all the more regrettable since younger artists such as Manet, who called him 'The painter's painter', have acknowledged their debt to him; also since we now know that the Louvre had been on the point of acquiring *The Rokeby Venus* when the National Gallery carried off this treasure in 1905.

At that time the keepers concentrated their efforts on the primitive painters who were just beginning to be rediscovered. The *Scenes from the Life of St George* (p 213), later identified as by the Catalan painter Martorell, were bought in 1904 and 1905, as well as *The blessing of the chasuble to St Ildefonso* (p 214) by a Hispano-Flemish artist from Castile, and three panels from a Valencian polyptych of the fifteenth century from the cathedral of Burgo de Osma. These pictures constitute, together with Huguet's altarpiece of *The flagellation of Christ* (p 213), painted for Barcelona Cathedral, a room of rare quality almost unmatched outside Spain.

The most recent acquisitions have provided a welcome variety in the collection by introducing significant works by seventeenth-century masters hitherto absent from the collections—Luis Tristan, Juan Valdes Leal, Vicente Carducho, Alonso Cano (p 218), and Jeronimo Jacinto Espinosa—or by evoking, albeit insufficiently, the eighteenth century, for example in Melendez's *Portrait of the artist* and *Still life*. Certain series have been completed: two canvases by Herrera from the Church of St Bonaventura in Seville, given by the Société des Amis du Louvre, have joined those by Zurbaran, while another episode from the cycle by Murillo from the Franciscan church at Seville has joined *The angels' kitchen*. Of all these treasures, the spectacular *Mass for the foundation of the Order of the Trinitarians* (p 219), painted by Carreño de Miranda in 1666 for the Trinitarian Church of Pamplona and given by the Comtesse de Caraman in 1964, is without doubt the most magnificent.

BERNARDO MARTORELL
Known in Barcelona from 1427 to 1452
The flagellation of St George, circa 1435
Wood 107 × 53 cm
Presented by the Société des Amis du Louvre, 1904

JAIME HUGUET
Valls, 1414—Barcelona, 1491
The Flagellation of Christ, between 1450 and 1460
Wood 106 × 210 cm
Purchased in 1967 with the help of the Société des Amis du
Louvre

Portuguese (?) master
Middle of the 15th century
Man with a glass of wine, circa 1450
Wood 63 × 44 cm
Purchased in 1906

MASTER OF ST ILDEFONSO
Castile, end of the 15th century
The blessing of the chasuble to St Ildefonso, circa 1490–1500
Wood 230 × 167 cm
Purchased in 1904

PEDRO BERRUGUETE
Paredes de Nava, *circa* 1450—Paredes de Nava, 1504
Plato, circa 1477
Wood 101 × 69 cm
Collection of the Marquis Campana, purchased in 1863

DOMENIKOS THEOTOCOPOULOS, called EL GRECO
Candia, 1541—Toledo, 1614
Christ on the Cross adored by donors, between 1576 and 1579
Canvas 260 × 171 cm
Purchased in 1908

FRANCISCO HERRERA THE ELDER
Seville, *circa* 1585—Madrid, after 1657
St Basil dictating his doctrine, circa 1639
Canvas 243 × 194 cm
Purchased in 1858

JOSÉ DE RIBERA
Jativa, 1591—Naples, 1652
The club-footed boy, 1642
Canvas 164 × 93 cm
Bequeathed by Louis La Caze, 1869

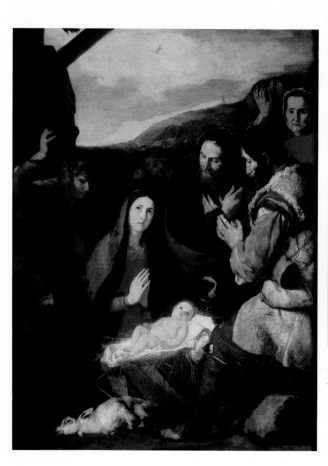

JOSÉ DE RIBERA
Jativa, 1591—Naples, 1652
The Adoration of the Shepherds, 1650
Canvas 239 × 181 cm
Given to the French Republic by the King of Naples in 1802 in
compensation for the paintings taken by Neapolitan troops at
St-Louis-des-Français

FRANCISCO DE ZURBARAN
Fuente de Cantos, 1598—Madrid, 1664
The lying-in-state of St Bonaventura, circa 1629
Canvas 245 × 220 cm
Purchased in 1858

The Louvre owns another painting by Zurbaran, *St Bonaventura at the Council of Lyon*, as well as two by Francisco de Herrera which belong to a series painted for the Franciscan college of St Bonaventura at Seville. During 'The Golden Age' the crusading faith of the great monastic orders multiplied the number of cycles illustrating the lives and miracles of popular saints. Through the low-key colouring and sombre subject matter, *tenebrismo*, derived from Caravaggio, Zurbaran here rediscovers the intense simplicity of the primitives.

217

ALONSO CANO
Granada, 1601—Granada, 1667
St John the Evangelist, 1636
Canvas 53 × 35 cm
Purchased in 1977

FRANCISCO COLLANTES
Madrid (?), *circa* 1599—Madrid (?), 1656
The Burning Bush, circa 1634
Canvas 116 × 163 cm
Collection of Louis XIV

JUAN CARREÑO DE MIRANDA
Gijon, 1614—Madrid, 1685
The mass for the foundation of the Order of the Trinitarians, 1666
Canvas 500 × 331 cm
Presented by the Comtesse de Caraman, 1964

BARTOLOMÉ ESTEBAN MURILLO
Seville, 1618—Seville, 1682
The Birth of the Virgin, between 1655 and 1658
Canvas 179 × 349 cm
Purchased in 1858

Bartolomé Esteban Murillo
Seville, 1618—Seville, 1682
The young beggar, circa 1650
Canvas 134 × 110 cm
Collection of Louis XVI, purchased in 1782

This work was painted at the beginning of Murillo's career. It is without doubt one of the first of the genre scenes in which he shows street urchins. Later his taste for the picturesque sometimes became merely anecdotal, but here the sincerity of his observation and the vigour of his technique place Murillo in the pure tradition of the Spanish *tenebrismo* of the young Velasquez and of Zurbaran. It is not surprising that painters like Courbet, Manet, and Monet admired such works.

Francisco Goya y Lucientes
Fuendetodos, 1746—Bordeaux, 1828
Ferdinand Guillemardet, 1798
Canvas 186 × 124 cm
Bequeathed by Louis Guillemardet, 1865

Francisco Goya y Lucientes
Fuendetodos, 1746—Bordeaux, 1828
Lady with a fan, circa 1805/10
Canvas 103 × 83 cm
Purchased in 1898

Luis Melendez
Naples, 1716—Madrid, 1780
Still life, circa 1760/70
Canvas 40 × 51 cm
Bequeathed by Emile Wauters, 1934

FRANCISCO GOYA Y LUCIENTES
Fuendetodos, 1746—Bordeaux, 1828
The Marquesa de la Solana, circa 1793
Canvas 181 × 122 cm
Presented by Carlos de Beistegui, 1942

The seventeenth and eighteenth centuries in Italy

It is to Louis XIV that we owe the foundation of the Italian and several other collections. However, some 'modern' Italian paintings had already entered the royal collection under Louis XIII—such as the *Public Felicity* painted for Marie de Médicis by Orazio Gentileschi during his stay in France in 1624–5 (p 226). It is also known that Guido Reni, and later Guercino, had been invited, but in vain, to come and work in France.

The taste for the Roman and Bolognese 'Grand Manner', which continued to inspire artists in France until the end of the eighteenth century, had spread amongst Parisian collectors by the mid-1600s. The Roman painter Giovanni Francesco Romanelli, having painted the ceiling of a gallery (now the Bibliothèque Nationale) for Cardinal Mazarin, was employed to decorate, in fresco, the Appartements d'Eté of Queen Anne of Austria in the Louvre (p 231). Another dazzling example of this predilection of contemporary French collectors was the gallery built in about 1634/45 by Louis-Phillipeaux de la Vrillière, and decorated with a series of vast canvases illustrating episodes of Roman history. He commissioned the most famous painters working in Rome and Bologna at the time—Guercino, Pietro da Cortona, Alessandro Turchi, and Carlo Maratta—to complete the series begun by Guido Reni's *The abduction of Helen* (p 230) and Poussin's *The schoolmaster of Falerii*. This series of ten great compositions was taken to the Louvre during the Revolution but has, unfortunately, since been dispersed. The Louvre has kept the paintings by Poussin, Reni, and Turchi, and one each by Guercino and Pietro da Cortona (p 231), but the others have been sent to various provincial museums and are replaced by copies.

The wholesale dispersal of the Mazarin and Jabach collections introduced several major seventeenth-century paintings to Louis XIV's collection, including the *Death of the Virgin* by Caravaggio (p 225) and the four paintings from the *Story of Hercules* by Guido Reni (p 230), which had come from Charles I's collection and previously from the Dukes of Mantua. Later, many paintings by the best-loved Bolognese artists—Carracci, Reni, Guercino, Domenichino, and Francesco Albani—were to adorn Louis XIV's collection, bought from, or given by, various French and Italian connoisseurs. Thus, in 1665, Prince Pamphili sent him from Rome *Hunting* and *Fishing* (p 227) by Annibale Carracci, as well as Caravaggio's *The fortune teller*; and André Le Nôtre, the King's gardener, left him his paintings by Albani in 1693. Amongst the works of other Italian schools in Louis XIV's collection were important paintings by Fetti, such as his *Melancholy* (p 232), Pier Francesco Mola, Lanfranco, Baciccia, and Castiglione.

Under Louis XV, the purchases from the estate of the Prince de Carignan in 1741 introduced other paintings by Pietro da Cortona, Maratta, and above all, Castiglione, one of the chief sources of inspiration for the French in the eighteenth century, including his *The expulsion of the merchants from the temple* and the *Adoration* (p 232). Systematic purchases made by d'Angiviller under Louis XVI, with a view to making the future Museum more comprehensive, also included Seicento paintings such as *The Raising of Lazarus* by Guercino (p 229) and works of the beginning of the eighteenth century such as *The expulsion of Heliodorus* by Solimena (p 233).

It is surprising that those responsible for the royal collections should have acquired so few works by contemporary Italian masters during the eighteenth century. Perhaps a trace of protectionism can be detected, justified by the good state of health in which contemporary French painting found itself? Nevertheless, the Venetian artists Sebastiano Ricci, and, especially, Rosalba Carriera and Giovanni Antonio Pellegrini had caused a sensation during their stays, in Paris in 1716 and in 1720. Today only their 'election pieces' at the Académie Royale de Peinture et de Sculpture, which entered the Louvre with the Academy collections during the Revolution, bear witness to their popularity. All trace of the painting sent to Louis xv by Tiepolo has been lost, and nothing remains of the Roman masters, despite their strong links with their French contemporaries and imitators resident in their city (links which were to lead to Neo-Classicism), save for the work of Gianpaolo Pannini, who was the protégé of the French ambassador, Cardinal de Polignac.

One masterpiece which fortuitously entered the collections of the Museum during the Revolution was the brilliant series of *Venetian festivals* by Francesco Guardi, illustrating the ceremonies of the Coronation of the Doge Alvise Mocenigo in 1763 (p 237–8). This cycle has now been dispersed, as several of the twelve canvases were sent to provincial museums during the Empire. However, a programme of exchanges, already begun, could ensure the reconstitution of the whole cycle.

The great Bolognese painters of the seventeenth century constituted one of the short-lived glories of the Musée Napoléon. Most of the paintings taken in Italy were returned in 1815, but some important canvases by Ludovico and Annibale Carracci, *The Virgin appears to St Hyacinth* (p 228) and *The Virgin appears to St Luke and St Catherine* (p 228), and by Guercino, *The patron saints of Modena* (p 229), remain in Paris and make the Emilian collection in the Louvre the most complete outside Bologna itself.

It is characteristic of the traditional French preference for the Bolognese painters that, with a few exceptions, such as Salvator Rosa (p 233), other Seicento Schools were excluded. Representation of Lombard, Neapolitan, and Florentine painting in this period was clearly insufficient and, in spite of more recent acquisitions, this lack of balance is still evident today. Even during the last century the seventeenth-century Italian collection increased little, while, on the other hand, the eighteenth-century section was consolidated. The *View of Santa Maria Salute* by Marieschi (then attributed to Canaletto) was acquired, and under Louis-Philippe important works by Panini, *The Last Supper* by Giovanni Battista Tiepolo in 1877, and later the sketch for a ceiling, *The triumph of religion*, by his son Gian Domenico were also acquired. In the last fifty years the Settecento schools collection has finally achieved some measure of uniformity. New works by the two Tiepolos (p 236), by Pellegrini, Sebastiano Ricci, and Giambattista Pittoni complete the Venetian collection, now dominated by Piazetta's monumental *Assumption* (p 235). Pietro Longhi, with his *The Presentation* (p 236) and Canaletto, from the Péreire and Lyon donations, at last have a place in the collection. The Neapolitan School is also better represented, by Francesco de Mura and Domenico Mondo, and the sombre realism of the northern Italian artists at the beginning of the eighteenth century is evoked by the almost uncanny expressionism of Magnasco's *'Le repas des bohémiens'* (p 234) or by the cosy intimacy of Crespi's *The flea* (p 234).

Michelangelo Merisi, called Caravaggio
Caravaggio, 1570 or 1571—Porto Ercole, 1610
The Death of the Virgin, 1605/06
Canvas 369 × 245 cm
Collection of Louis XIV, purchased in 1671

ORAZIO GENTILESCHI
Pisa, 1563—London, 1639
Public Felicity triumphant over dangers, circa 1624/5
Canvas 268 × 170 cm
Collection of Marie de Médicis

MICHELANGELO MERISI, called CARAVAGGIO
Caravaggio, 1570 or 1571—Porto Ercole, 1610
The fortune teller, circa 1594/5
Canvas 99 × 131 cm
Collection of Louis XIV, purchased in 1665

ORAZIO GENTILESCHI
Pisa, 1563—London, 1639
Rest on the Flight, circa 1628
Canvas 158 × 225 cm
Collection of Louis XIV, purchased in
1671

ANNIBALE CARRACCI
Bologna, 1560—Rome, 1609
Fishing, circa 1585/8
Canvas 135 × 253 cm
Collection of Louis XIV, purchased in 1665

DOMENICO ZAMPIERI, called DOMENICHINO
Bologna, 1581—Rome, 1641
Landscape with Erminia and the shepherds, circa 1620
Canvas 123 × 181 cm
Collection of Louis XIV, purchased in 1661

ANNIBALE CARRACCI
Bologna, 1560—Rome, 1609
The Virgin appears to St Luke and St Catherine, 1592
Canvas 401 × 226 cm
From the Cathedral of Reggio Emilia
Entered in 1797

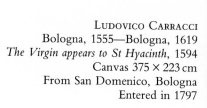

LUDOVICO CARRACCI
Bologna, 1555—Bologna, 1619
The Virgin appears to St Hyacinth, 1594
Canvas 375 × 223 cm
From San Domenico, Bologna
Entered in 1797

GIAN-FRANCESCO BARBIERI, called GUERCINO
Cento, 1591—Bologna, 1666
The patron saints of the town of Modena, circa 1651/2
Canvas 332 × 230 cm
From the Ducal Gallery, Modena
Entered in 1797

GIAN-FRANCESCO BARBIERI, called GUERCINO
Cento, 1591—Bologna, 1666
The Raising of Lazarus, circa 1619
Canvas 199 × 233 cm
Collection of Louis XVI, purchased in 1785

GUIDO RENI
Bologna, 1575—Bologna, 1642
The abduction of Helen, 1631
Canvas 253 × 265 cm
Seized during the French Revolution
(collection of the Duc de Penthièvre)

GUIDO RENI
Bologna, 1575—Bologna, 1642
Deianeira and the centaur Nessus, 1621
Canvas 259 × 193 cm
Collection of Louis XIV, purchased in 1662

PIETRO BERETTINO DA CORTONA
Cortona, 1596—Rome, 1669
Romulus and Remus given shelter by
Faustulus, circa 1643
Canvas 251 × 266 cm
Seized during the French Revolution
(collection of the Duc de Penthièvre)

GIOVANNI FRANCESCO ROMANELLI
Rome, *circa* 1610—Rome, 1662
Diana and Actaeon, circa 1655
Mural painting 450 × 355 cm
Section of the ceiling of the Petite Galerie in the Louvre

GIOVANNI-BATTISTA GAULLI, called BACICCIA
Genoa, 1639—Rome, 1709
The preaching of St John the Baptist, circa 1690
Canvas 181 × 172 cm
Collection of Louis XIV, entered before 1695

GIOVANNI BENEDETTO CASTIGLIONE
Genoa, *circa* 1611 (?)—Mantua, 1663 or 1665
The Adoration of the Shepherds, circa 1645/50
Copper 68 × 52 cm
Collection of Louis XV, purchased in 1742

DOMENICO FETTI
Rome, *circa* 1589—Venice, 1623
Melancholy, circa 1620
Canvas 168 × 128 cm
Collection of Louis XIV, purchased in 1685

SALVATOR ROSA
Naples, 1615—Rome, 1673
The shade of Samuel appears to Saul, 1668
Canvas 275 × 191 cm
Collection of Louis XIV, purchased
before 1683

FRANCESCO SOLIMENA
Pagani, 1657—Naples, 1747
The expulsion of Heliodorus, circa 1723/5
Canvas 150 × 200 cm
Collection of Louis XVI, purchased in
1786

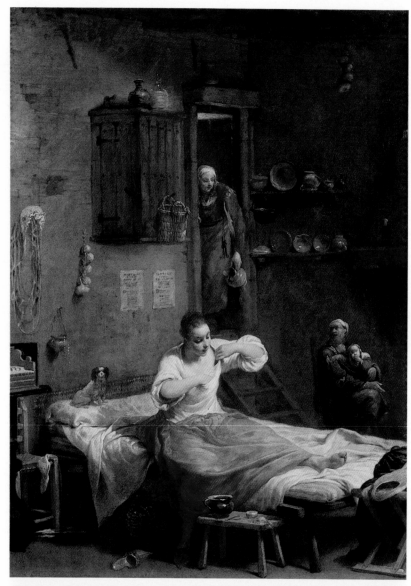

GIUSEPPE MARIA CRESPI
Bologna, 1665—Bologna, 1747
The flea, circa 1720/5
Canvas 54 × 40 cm
Presented by the Société des Amis du
Louvre, 1970

ALESSANDRO MAGNASCO
Genoa, 1667—Genoa, 1749
A toast to the betrothed couple, known as
'Le repas des bohémiens', circa 1730/40
Canvas 86 × 118 cm
Presented by M et Mme Christian
Lazard, 1927

GIAMBATTISTA PIAZZETTA
Venice, 1683—Venice, 1754
The Assumption of the Virgin, 1735
Canvas 517 × 245 cm
From the church of the Germanic order
of Sachsenhausen, near Frankfurt
Entered in 1796

This painting was commissioned from
Piazzetta by the Prince Elector of
Cologne to decorate the High Altar of
the Church of the Teutonic Order at
Sachsenhausen. It is a dazzling example
of the great vertical compositions
invented by the Romans and Venetians
and based on a rhythmic ascending
movement which was later adopted by
German Baroque architects. In his
earlier works Piazzetta had tended to use
darker colours, but here he lightens his
palette while retaining the solid power
of the forms.

GIOVANNI BATTISTA TIEPOLO
Venice, 1696—Madrid, 1770
The Last Supper, circa 1745/50
Canvas 79 × 88 cm
Purchased in 1877

PIETRO LONGHI
Venice, 1702—Venice, 1785
The Presentation, circa 1740
Canvas 64 × 53 cm
Bestowed by the Office des Biens Privés, 1950

GIANDOMENICO TIEPOLO
Venice, 1727—Venice, 1804
Carnival scene, circa 1745/50
Canvas 805 × 1105 cm
Bequeathed by Alexandre-Robert Le
Roux de Villers, 1938

Francesco Guardi
Venice, 1712—Venice, 1792
The Doge on the Bucentaur at San Niccolò del Lido, circa 1766/70
Canvas 67 × 100 cm
Seized during the French Revolution (collection of Pestre de Seneffe)

This painting belongs to a series of twelve canvases, almost all in the Louvre, which recount the various episodes in the election of Doge Alvise Mocenigo of Venice in 1763. In reporting this event Guardi was inspired by engravings after that other master of the Venetian view, *veduta*, Antonio Canaletto. An observant and picturesque record of the traditional Venetian festival, which was part official ceremony and part popular rejoicing, this series attests to the pictorial verve of Guardi and to his sensitivity to the most fleeting atmospheric effects, worthy of the Impressionists over a century later.

FRANCESCO GUARDI
Venice, 1712—Venice, 1792
*Audience granted by the Doge to the
ambassadors in the Sala del Collegio of the
Doges' Palace, circa 1766/70*
Canvas 66 × 100 cm
Seized during the French Revolution
(collection of Pestre de Seneffe)

GIOVANNI PAOLO PANINI
Piacenza, 1691—Rome, 1764
*A musical fête given by the Cardinal de la
Rochefoucauld at the Theatre Argentina,
Rome, on 15 July 1747 in honour of the
marriage of the Dauphin of France*, 1747
Canvas 204 × 247 cm
Collection of Louis-Philippe

The Germanic countries

The Louvre could not claim, any more than any other museum outside Germany, to illustrate fully the long history of painting in the Germanic countries. At least the collection has some strong points, however uneven it remains in its overall coverage. These are perhaps best outlined chronologically rather than in order of their entry to the collections as elsewhere. Firstly, a small group of paintings in the International Gothic style are of merit. Curiously, several of these small pictures once passed as French, at a time between the World Wars when enthusiasm for the rediscovered French primitives caused their output to 'increase' at the expense of German and Spanish painters. The panel of *The Virgin with a rose garland with Otto von Hohenstein, Bishop of Merseburg* of *circa* 1400 is now attributed to a Saxon artist, and that of *The Virgin at her writing-desk* of *circa* 1420 to an Austrian artist. The small polyptych called the *Chapelle Cardon*, bequeathed by the Belgian collector, Cardon, in 1921 is attributed to an artist of the Lower Rhine. A *Virgin and Child* belonging to the most refined courtly Gothic style of central Europe came from Bohemia in the second quarter of the fifteenth century.

The important collection of the early masters working in Cologne begins with a minute *Miracle of St Voult*, which was also once attributed to a French artist but was in fact painted in about 1440 by a follower of Stefan Lochner. This collection represents the work of most of the anonymous masters of the end of the fifteenth century who lived in the rich Cologne centre of painting. They include the Master of St Bartholomew, whose monumental *Descent from the Cross* (p 241) was in Paris from the sixteenth century; the Master of the Holy Family, whose *Altarpiece of the Seven Joys of Mary* (p 241) was purchased in 1912; the Master of the Legend of St Bruno; the Master of St Severinus, whose *The Presentation in the Temple* was a gift of the Société des Amis du Louvre in 1972; and the Master of St Ursula, whose two *Scenes from the life of St Ursula* were part of a cycle dispersed among several museums. Although born in Cologne, the Master of St Ursula also seems to have painted the *Pietà*, which was undertaken around 1500 in Paris for the church of Saint-Germain-des-Prés and which has a delicate view of Paris in the background. Finally, the last painter of the Cologne School during the Renaissance, Barthel Bruyn, is represented by the double portrait of the large Gail Family, purchased in 1916.

The other fifteenth-century German schools are hardly represented at all; a visit to the museum of Dijon will find a varied collection of German primitives in France. Among several panels which are in the collection, the following are outstanding: the *Annunciation* with two *Saints* by the Ulm master, Barthel Zeitblom, given by the Marchesa Arconati-Visconti in 1916, and a *St George rescuing the Princess* by a master of the Upper Rhine at the end of the fifteenth century. A mysterious *Portrait of a woman*, bought in 1920 and called *The Delphic Sibyl*, would seem to be a fifteenth-century painting reflecting the influence of the Master of Flémalle, although it was earlier attributed to Ludger Tom Ring, a painter working in Munster in the mid-sixteenth century.

Dürer and Holbein dominate the collection of great Renaissance masters. The *Self portrait* of 1493 by Dürer (p 242), purchased by the Louvre in 1922, is undoubtedly the first independent self-portrait painted north of the Alps (excluding that of Fouquet, painted on enamel and also in the Louvre). The Cabinet des Dessins already had two canvases by the artist: the masterly *Portrait of an old man*, dated 1520, and the curiously bearded *Head of a youth* of 1527.

The five Holbein portraits are amongst the glories of the Museum and entered the royal collection in the seventeenth century. The *Portrait of Erasmus* (p 245) was a gift from Charles I to his brother-in-law Louis XIII in exchange for Leonardo's *John the Baptist* (which later returned to Louis XIV). The other paintings—*William Warham, Henry Wyatt, Nicolas Kratzer* (p 245), and *Anne of Cleves*—had belonged to the Earl of Arundel, a passionate collector and inspiration and rival of Charles I, and were bought for the collection of Louis XIV at the Jabach sale. From the Mazarin collection Louis XIV acquired another masterpiece of the German Renaissance, a table painted for Cardinal Albert of Brandenburg by Hans Sebald Beham with minute and fanciful *Scenes from the life of David* (p 246).

The collection also contains a group of paintings by Lucas Cranach which include a *Venus* purchased in 1806 (p 243) and a *Portrait of a young girl* bought in 1910 (p 243). The other works of the first half of the sixteenth century form a more disparate group, from the *Adoration of the Magi* by Ulrich Apt of Augsburg, purchased in 1807, to the allegory of *The knight, the young girl, and Death* by Hans Baldung Grien (p 244). The recent purchase of Wolf Huber's *Lamentation* (p 244) brings to mind the lyricism and visual liberties of the masters of the Danube School, now fashionable once again.

The seventeenth century in Germany, whose diversity has been revealed in different exhibitions, is represented only by some powerful and poetic still lifes by such artists as Georg Flegel and Gottfried von Wedig. A series of portraits represents the eighteenth century in Germany and Austria, which deserves to be better known. They range from psychological studies, in the works of Balthasar Denner and Christian Seybold and official effigies by Mengs, to the international type of the elegant *fin-de-siècle* portrait in the works of Angelica Kauffmann and Anton Graff, whose formula is re-echoed in the work of Johann Baptist Lampi and the Russian artists Levitski and Borovikovski.

Nineteenth-century painting in the Germanic countries figures in the national collection only in the works of the second half of the century by Mackart, Bocklin, and Liebermann, which are destined for the Musée d'Orsay. The greatest German painter of the beginning of the century, and one of the geniuses of European Romanticism, Caspar David Friedrich, is still an isolated figure in the collection: the *Tree of crows* (p 246) was purchased for the Louvre in 1975.

MASTER OF THE HOLY FAMILY
Active in Cologne between 1475 and *circa* 1510
Altarpiece of the Seven Joys of Mary, circa 1480
Wood 127 × 182 cm
Purchased in 1912

MASTER OF ST BARTHOLOMEW
Active in Cologne between 1475 and 1510
The Descent from the Cross, circa 1500/05
Wood 227 × 210 cm
From the church of the Val de Grâce, Paris

ALBRECHT DÜRER
Nuremberg, 1471—Nuremberg, 1528
Self portrait, 1493
Parchment mounted on canvas 56 × 44 cm
Purchased in 1922

LUCAS CRANACH
Kronach, 1472—Weimar, 1553
*Portrait presumed to be of Magdalena Luther, daughter of Martin
Luther, circa* 1540 (?)
Wood 39 × 25 cm
Purchased in 1910

LUCAS CRANACH
Kronach, 1472—Weimar, 1553
Venus, 1529
Wood 33 × 26 cm
Entered in 1806

Like Rembrandt and van Gogh, Dürer often made studies of
his own face. He was one of the very first European painters to
show this tendency, which represented a realisation of the
individuality of the artist, who had previously been regarded
simply as a craftsman. This painting is the first of Dürer's self-
portraits, and was painted at the age of twenty-two when he
was travelling in Germany before settling in Nuremburg in
1494. The plant held by the artist obviously has an allegorical
significance; it may be an emblem of conjugal fidelity in
reference to his betrothal to Agnes Frey, or alternatively a
symbol of the suffering of Christ.

243

HANS BALDUNG GRIEN
Gmünd, 1484/5—Strasbourg, 1545
The knight, the young girl, and Death, circa 1505
Wood 355 × 296 cm
Purchased in 1924

German School, 15th century (?)
Portrait of a woman, called *The Delphic Sibyl*
Wood 44 × 31 cm
Attributed to Ludger Tom Ring the Elder
Purchased in 1920

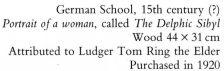

WOLF HUBER
Feldkirch (?), *circa* 1485—Passau, 1553
The Lamentation of Christ, 1524
Wood 105 × 86 cm
Purchased in 1968

HANS HOLBEIN
Augsburg, 1497—London, 1543
Nicholas Kratzer, 1528
Wood 83 × 67 cm
Collection of Louis XIV, purchased in 1671

HANS HOLBEIN
Augsburg, 1497—London, 1543
Erasmus, 1523
Wood 42 × 32 cm
Collection of Louis XIV, purchased in 1671

HANS SEBALD BEHAM
Nuremberg, 1500—Frankfurt, 1550
Scenes from the life of David, 1534
Painted table, wood 128 × 131 cm
Collection of Louis XIV

CASPAR DAVID FRIEDRICH
Greifswald, 1774—Dresden, 1840
The tree of crows, circa 1822
Canvas 59 × 74 cm
Purchased in 1975

Great Britain

ritish painting is very unevenly represented in most of the great
museums outside the English-speaking countries, and is often
considered to be the poor relation in European art. While the
Louvre does not offer a sufficiently varied or detailed illustration of the
various trends of the British school it is, to a certain extent, the exception
to this rule, as its collection is quite extensive. It begins with a good
William Scrots, the *Portrait of Edward VI*, and continues until the end of the
nineteenth century (the paintings from the second half of the century, from
the Pre-Raphaelites onwards, will be shown at the Musée d'Orsay). It is
true that figures of the eminence of Hogarth and Richard Wilson or of
William Blake and Samuel Palmer are still absent, but a fair number of
other very important painters, from Allan Ramsay to Turner, are
represented by works which are of artistic value even if they are not always
exceptional or sufficiently numerous.

With the exception of the purchase of a small painting by Bonington,
François I and the Duchesse d'Etampes in 1849, and that of his *Parterre d'eau at
Versailles* in 1872, as well as two paintings by Constable (p 253), the
collection was built up in two distinct stages: during the years 1880–1910
and since the Second World War.

The first stage corresponded to a great vogue for English painting—or at
least a certain view of English painting—which was upheld in Paris by
journals such as *l'Art* (later *Les Arts*) and important dealers such as Charles
Sedelmeyer. The organisation of an exhibition at Bagatelle (1905) and,
above all, the large number of English paintings which entered the great
Parisian collections of the time, bore witness to this fashion. One of these,
the collection created with such enthusiasm by Camille Groult, was to
become as famous for its Gainsboroughs and Turners as for its Watteaus. It
was in this fervently pro-British climate that the Louvre purchased, in
Paris or London, some of its most remarkable portraits, for example *Mr
and Mrs Angerstein* (p 252) by Lawrence in 1896, *Sir John Stanley* by Ramsey
in 1897, and *Captain Robert May* by Raeburn in 1908. At the same time the
Museum received a number of canvases which, we can now admit, say
more for the generosity of their anglophile donors than for the merits of
their presumed artists. Happily, certain paintings of the highest quality
were also given at this time: the famous *Master Hare* by Reynolds (p 249) in
Baron Alphonse de Rothschild Bequest of 1905, and several works by
Bonington. Soon after the Second World War the Louvre acquired a
number of pictures which recall the taste of the great French collectors at
the end of the last century for the elegance and pictorial verve of the best
English portraitists of the eighteenth century: the sumptuous *Portrait of
Lady Alston* by Gainsborough (p 250), a masterpiece of the Bath period
given in 1947 by the heirs of Baron Robert de Rothschild; his delightful
Conversation in a park (p 249), a rare early work which may be a self-
portrait of the artist and his wife; and the *Portrait of Charles William Bell* by
Lawrence.

In the last thirty years or so the keepers of the Department of Paintings
have tried to complete this heritage more systematically. On the one hand,
they have strengthened the representation of certain artists, like Constable

(who was so important at the birth of French romanticism for the visual liberation of the artist confronted by nature), with his *View in the park at Helmingham* bought in 1948 and *View of Salisbury* (p 253) from the Percy Moore Turner bequest of 1952, and Lawrence, with his presumed *Portrait of the Angerstein children*, purchased by the Société des Amis du Louvre. On the other hand, they, have attempted to fill the most lamentable gaps. The absence of Turner, perhaps the greatest of English artists, had long been regretted as he was linked to France by his admiration for Claude Lorrain. He is now represented in the Louvre by one of his late works (p 253) in which, typically, the dissolution of form gives the appearance of an unfinished painting.

The history of English painting in the eighteenth century has changed considerably in the last thirty years, inasmuch as the scale of values which determined it has altered. Artists like Stubbs and Joseph Wright of Derby who had been neglected for a long time have now regained their rightful place in the hierarchy of excellence, relegating fashionable portraitists, whose technique was weak and appeal superficial, to the background. We have also rediscovered the sharp simplicity of Zoffany's conversation pieces and, at the opposite extreme, the heated visions of the anglicised Swiss, Fuseli (p 251). The recent purchases of a *View of the Lake of Nemi* by Wright (p 249), the *Portrait of the Reverend Randall Burroughes with his son* by Zoffany, and Fuseli's *Lady Macbeth* (p 251) mark the beginning of a programme of acquisitions which aims to diversify the Louvre's representation of the complex and rich period of the late eighteenth century.

Similarly, an opening has been made into nineteenth-century painting in the United States with the purchase in 1975 of the Romantic *Cross in solitude* painted in 1848 by Thomas Cole. The American artists of the turn of the century, Thomas Eakins, Winslow Homer, and Whistler—whose portrait *The artist's mother* (p 254) is one of the most popular images of Anglo Saxon painting—will be shown at the Musée d'Orsay.

JOSHUA REYNOLDS
Plympton, 1723—London, 1792
Master Hare, circa 1788/9
Canvas 77 × 63 cm
Bequeathed by Baron Alphonse de Rothschild, 1905

THOMAS GAINSBOROUGH
Sudbury, 1727—London, 1788
Conversation in a park, circa 1746/7
Canvas 73 × 68 cm
Presented by M. Pierre Bordeaux-Groult, 1952

JOSEPH WRIGHT, called WRIGHT OF DERBY
Derby, 1734—Derby, 1797
View of the Lake of Nemi, circa 1790/5
Canvas 105 × 128 cm
Purchased in 1970

Thomas Gainsborough
Sudbury, 1727—London, 1788
Lady Alston, circa 1760/5
Canvas 226 × 168 cm
Presented by the heirs of Baron Robert de Rothschild

This work dates from Gainsborough's mature period, when
he resided in Bath as a fashionable portraitist of the
aristocracy. Following the elegant van Dyck tradition, he
places the model in a broad landscape background. However,
the strong contrasts of the lighting of the figure and the
flashing effect achieved on the silk of her dress against the
deep, impenetrable forest behind her, make this mysterious
and poetic portrait a totally original work.

HENRY RAEBURN
Stockbridge, 1756—Edinburgh, 1823
Young girl holding flowers, circa 1798/1800 (?)
Canvas 92 × 71 cm
Bequeathed by Mme Pierre Lebaudy, 1962

JOHANN HEINRICH FUSELI
Zurich, 1741—London, 1825
Lady Macbeth, 1784
Canvas 221 × 160 cm
Purchased in 1970

THOMAS LAWRENCE
Bristol, 1769—London, 1830
Mr and Mrs Julius Angerstein, 1792
Canvas 252 × 160 cm
Purchased in 1896

JOHN CONSTABLE
East Bergholt, 1776—London, 1837
View of Salisbury, circa 1820 (?)
Canvas 35 × 51 cm
Bequeathed by Percy Moore Turner,
1952

RICHARD PARKES BONINGTON
Arnold, 1802—London, 1828
The parterre d'eau at Versailles, circa 1826 (?)
Canvas 43 × 54 cm
Purchased in 1872

JOSEPH MALLORD WILLIAM TURNER
London, 1775—London, 1851
Landscape with a river and a bay in the background,
circa 1835/40
Canvas 93 × 123 cm
Purchased in 1967

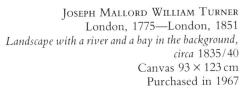

JAMES MacNeill Whistler
Lowell, 1834—London, 1903
The artist's mother, between 1867 and 1872
Canvas 144 × 162 cm
Purchased in 1891 for the Musée du Luxembourg

It is no doubt because the artist has convincingly suggested a universal image in this portrayal of his mother, that this picture has become one of the most popular of all Anglo-Saxon painting. In his attempt to be faithful in this quiet and intimate portrait, Whistler returns to the realism which had marked his early work in Paris. However, as the sub-title ('Arrangement in grey and black') indicates, the picture is also a tonal composition which shows the artist's admiration for Velasquez.

Index